Aegean Flavours

First published in the UK, US and Australia in 2014 by Jacqui Small LLP
74–77 White Lion Street
London N1 9PF

First edition: İstanbul, April 2010

Editor **Adrian Higgs**
English Translation **Adrian Higgs**
Photography **Orhan Cem Çetin**
Book Design **Esen Karol**
Publisher **Jacqui Small**
Managing Editor **Lydia Halliday**
Production **Maeve Healy**

ISBN 978 1 909342 48 4

A catalogue record for this book is available from the British Library.

2016 2015 2014
10 9 8 7 6 5 4 3 2 1

Printed in China

Didem Şenol Tiryakioğlu

Aegean Flavours

A Culinary Celebration of Turkish Cuisine from Hot Smoked Lamb to Baked Figs

jacqui small

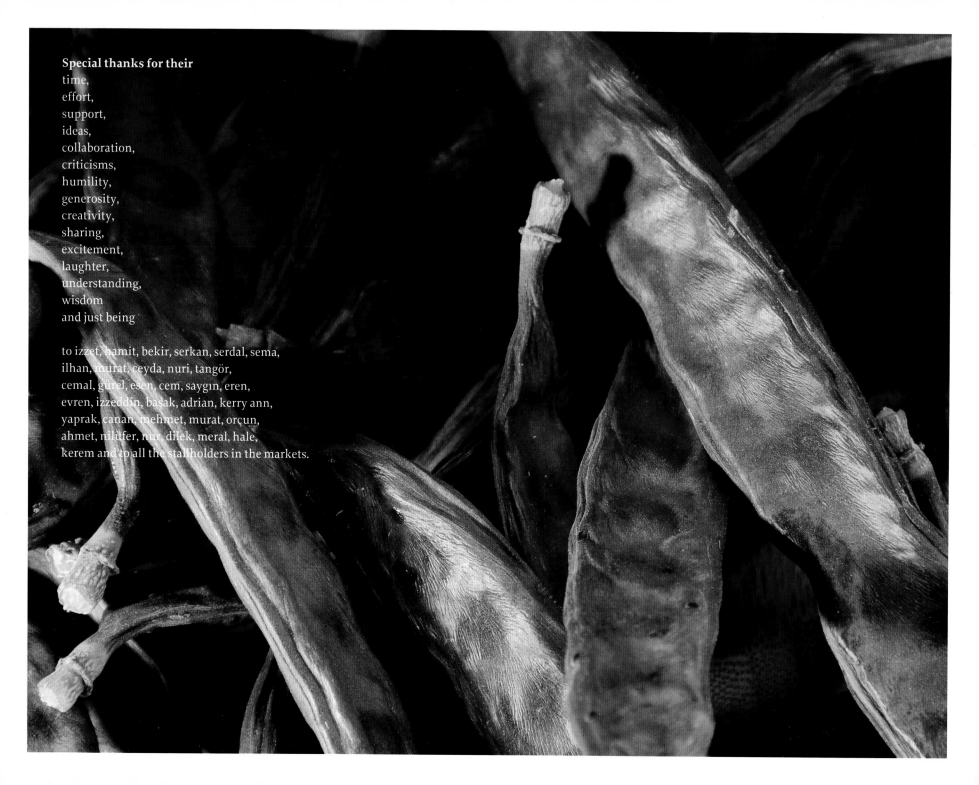

Special thanks for their
time,
effort,
support,
ideas,
collaboration,
criticisms,
humility,
generosity,
creativity,
sharing,
excitement,
laughter,
understanding,
wisdom
and just being

to izzet, hamit, bekir, serkan, serdal, sema,
ilhan, murat, ceyda, nuri, tangör,
cemal, gürel, esen, cem, saygın, eren,
evren, izzeddin, başak, adrian, kerry ann,
yaprak, canan, mehmet, murat, orçun,
ahmet, nilüfer, nur, dilek, meral, hale,
kerem and to all the stallholders in the markets.

I DELIGHT in rising at the crack of dawn to go to market, to see and smell the myriad fruits and vegetables that are in season, and to drink tea and chat with the stallholders. I love entering my kitchen in the dim morning light when all are asleep and the scents of cleaning supplies and the idle gas stove mingle. Dull though a dark kitchen may seem to many, after bringing it to life by turning on the oven and setting water to boil, I quickly transform it into a fragrant, dynamic, bright place full of colourful fruits and vegetables, fish, meat, flour, sugar and herbs and spices. Then, at the end of a long day, I stay up late going over each and every order chit until my feet go numb, and then I sit down and rest, eating crackers and cheese and listening to the kitchen crew's lengthy critique of the day.

So how do I prepare meals? I consider who I'm cooking for and I envisage the table setting. Menus that I plan for a large family on a cold winter night will differ greatly from the one I prepare for a romantic couple having an intimate barefoot dinner by the sea. A menu for a business luncheon will have nothing in common with the food I prepare for my rambunctious friends.

I always use ingredients that are in season and I also take into account the temperature, breeze and humidity. Light and refreshing desserts suit a close summer evening in a way that a rich, highly aromatic dinner suits rainy autumn nights. In preparing this book, I had great fun revisiting the 11 Aegean markets I write about, and observing the seasonal changes in the colour of the produce. Havran, Urla, Alaçatı, Tire, Milas, Yalıkavak, Muğla, Ula, Marmaris, Bozburun, Datça: each has its unique flavour, smell and texture. Meals cooked with fresh ingredients in season are easy to prepare; there is no need to tart them up since natural foods are very attractive and tasty.

Given the right ingredients, I turn my attention to the balance of flavours. Our tongues detect four main taste groups: salty, sweet, sour and spicy. Mixing any of these groups will increase flavour. Balancing the acid in onion with sugar or the sweetness of caramel with salt makes our meals tastier. The temperature and texture of a dish follow this balance; the greater the variety of texture, the more pleasure we get from our food. Chopped walnuts over a soft, smooth winter pumpkin dessert balance the sweetness of the pumpkin and extend the time we retain it, with all its flavour, in our mouths. So I use breadcrumbs, almonds, caramelized walnuts, currants, pistachios and other such ingredients in many of the recipes I present here. They all contribute to more engaging and delicious dishes.

A chef has to become skilled at designing menus with the totality of the dining experience in mind. Passing from a rich dish to a bland one is an invitation to disappointment, so I graduate the dishes on my menus according to the intensity of their flavours and their richness.

Technique is of equal importance to anything I've mentioned above. I have gone into some detail about my techniques in this book. When should I add salt? At what temperature should the chicken be served? In which direction should I cut the meat? The answers to these and similar questions all affect the outcome, so it is worth getting it right. The most effective check on how you are doing is to taste the food habitually at every stage of preparation: raw, while cooking and before serving. I believe that the first step to preparing good food is developing your sense of taste, so I leave it to the reader to decide how much salt or pepper to add—taste the food while you are preparing it and decide. Following my recipes will make your job easier, but by all means experiment with different herbs and spices. Even if the book offers various options, you may create more.

After writing this book I loved the coast even more: the markets and the stallholders, the roads, the fields, the air, the colours, the children, even the dogs and cats—all enrich one's joie de vivre. It is a great pleasure to journey around the south Aegean, savour the enjoyment of exploring markets for fresh produce to throw in your bag, delight in the plethora of produce and tastes found in this corner of Turkey and come to appreciate the difference between pink tomatoes, those grown near Çannakale in the north of the region and the succulent ones from Datça way down in the south. One ingredient, yet so many flavours, all within this small region.

And so I return, refreshed, each morning to my kitchen in the faint light of morning to renew the adventure. I hope my book inspires you to do the same.

Didem Şenol Tiryakioğlu

HAVRAN 16 – 37

URLA 40 – 61

ALAÇATI ÖDEMİŞ 64 – 81

 **TİRE** **84–105**

 **MİLAS** **108–131**

 **YALIKAVAK** **134–151**

BOZBURUN 232–251

DATÇA 254–277

POULTRY DISHES

- Whole roast chicken with fresh oregano, 20
- Grilled chicken with green olive sauce and sorrel salad, 112
- Free-range chicken and *köy eriştesi* soup with *süzme* yoghurt, 186
- Quail with rosemary and mushrooms, 184
- *Köy ekmeği* stuffed with *Çerkez tavuğu* and sun-dried tomatoes, 208
- Crispy chicken with spicy honey sauce, 170

MEAT DISHES

- Slow-roasted oxtail, 25
- Roasted rack of lamb and pureed potatoes with olives, 26
- Rump of lamb marinated in molasses and served with roast potatoes with rosemary, 30
- Lamb stew with cumin seeds and *günbalı*, 42
- Lamb shanks with chickpeas, 160
- Hot-smoked lamb loins with mustard sauce and caramelized onion, 166
- Fillet with red wine sauce seasoned with savory, 182
- Aubergine stuffed with stewed lamb, 266
- Marinated lamb spare ribs, 270
- Grilled beef tongue and potato salad with capers, 223
- Sautéed kidney with fresh oregano, 94
- Grilled fillet sautéed with beetroot stalks, 220

SEA FOOD DISHES

- Sautéed squid with cannellini beans, 102
- Red snapper with baked cos lettuce, 92
- Spicy sautéed octopus with fresh oregano, 44
- Sole with oregano and *hoplatma patates*, 80
- Whiting with olive oil and fennel, 110
- Sautéed monkfish with green apple and fennel salad, 120
- Mussels steamed in *Rakı*, 128
- Dusky grouper baked in milk, 130
- Baked seafood with orange and dill, 138
- Leerfish schnitzel and crushed potatoes with herbs, 142
- Sardines wrapped in grape leaves with turnip green pesto and tomato salad with sumac, 226
- White grouper with samphire sautéed with garlic and lemon peel, 234
- Coriander and gurnard fishcakes, 202
- Caramelized sea bass, baked figs and herbs with crushed almond dressing, 256
- Baked sea bream with capers and olives, 274
- Grilled crayfish with olive oil, rocket and parsley dressing, 246
- Grilled squid with white cheese and char-grilled aubergine stuffing, 240
- White grouper on sautéed artichokes, 158
- Grilled red mullet and warm cannellini bean puree with lemon rind, 276

DESSERTS

- Ice cream with dates and cognac, 86
- Fig tart, 104
- Sweet *lor peyniri* with black mulberry jam, 100
- Minted melon julep, 48
- Hazelnut cake with warm chocolate sauce, 54
- Caramelized rice pudding with *sakiz*, 68
- Baked pumpkin with vanilla sauce, 116
- Meringue with bergamot-flavoured chocolate sauce and ice cream, 150
- Chocolate truffles with chestnuts, 168
- Grilled fruit with *kaymak* and walnuts, 172
- *Kağıt helva* with berries and ice cream, 216

BREAKFAST DISHES

- Jasmine flower fruit salad, 228
- Eggy toast with peach and apricot sauté, 190
- Candied quince with *tulum peyniri*, 162
- Flavoured butters: dried tomatoes and walnuts, dill and lemon, honey and lavender, 164
- Sour cherry and cinnamon jam, 52
- White cherry and coriander jam, 34
- Bread rolls baked in a wood-fired oven, 250
- *Hurma* olives marinated with lavender, 58

HAVRAN

HAVRAN

ALAÇATI

URLA

TİRE

MİLAS

MUĞLA

YALIKAVAK

ULA

MARMARİS

DATÇA

BOZBURUN

ONE OF THE WONDERS of motorcycling through the Kaz Dağları Mountains of the southern Troad is the plethora of natural scents. Along with the fragrances, the vistas and temperatures change as you pass through olive groves and discover villages nestled among chestnut and oak trees. On one of these trips, we came upon the Havran market, which is set up on Fridays and where we spent a colourful day. I was enthralled by the sacks full of walnuts, home-made molasses and the best pomegranate syrup I could ever have imagined. Havran market makes you want to taste everything you see—especially the cheeses. They are so appetizing that, faced with the opportunity, we tasted the region's famous tulum peyniri cheese (from sheep's milk), testi peyniri (local cheese aged underground in an earthenware pot) and kelle peyniri (hard sheep's cheese)—each more delicious than the last.

In the autumn, dozens of varieties of olives and all kinds of olive oil from near and far fill the marketplace. If you want to put aside your own stock of olives in brine, you can buy newly picked, unprocessed olives at the Havran market. Passing between the stalls, I selected the ugliest pomegranates I could find in the belief that the uglier the exterior of a pomegranate, the tastier it is.

We leave the market, with its pungent earthen fragrance, and take off down the road to Edremit. We reach Edremit Square a half hour later and have a delicious kadın budu köfte (meatballs) for lunch.

Then we wend our way towards Çamlıbel, Adatepe and Behramkale villages, near the coast. We arrive in Behramkale at sunset and snack on this and that bought from the fishing boats anchored along the coast. On the return trip, I go slowly, attentive to the historical landscape.

The next morning, we get up early and restart our journey, making sure to stop by the Buğday Derneği (Wheat Association). We investigate local seeds and visit hilltop villages in the vicinity. We go through Ezine, where we buy aged white cheese made the year before. I fill my backpack and whatever other space I can find in my other bags with cans of white cheese and, paying no heed to the rain, we quickly make our way toward Bandırma.

Compared with other areas in the Aegean, there is a prevailing serenity on this peninsula, which is one of the reasons I like travelling during the windy, rainy olive season of autumn. Dreaming of delicious meals cooked at length, we return to the city. I have this urge to cook legumes, grains and meat dishes with plenty of sauce. The cool weather is reflected in my meals. Meals that linger on the palate and are richer and more filling than those of summer are the order of the day.

Dishes capturing the flavours of Havran market

- Barley pilaf with lemon rind, 18
- Whole roast chicken with fresh oregano, 20
- Spinach salad with pomegranate, 22
- Slow-roasted oxtail, 25
- Roasted rack of lamb and pureed potatoes with olives, 26
- Fried courgette flowers filled with *lor peyniri*, 28
- Rump of lamb marinated in molasses and served with roast potatoes with rosemary, 30
- Rocket salad with pear and *kelle peyniri*, 32
- White cherry and coriander jam, 34
- Spinach and Ezine cheese pizza, 36

Barley pilaf with lemon rind

250 g (9 oz/2½ cups) barley
2 litres (68 fl oz/2 quarts)
    cold water
100 g (3.5 oz/1 stick) butter
2 spring onions (scallions)
500-600 ml (18-20 fl oz/
    2¼-2½ cups) chicken
    stock
Grated rind of ½ lemon
Salt
Freshly ground black pepper

4 SERVINGS

The reason why I like barley pilaf is its unique texture in my mouth. We serve barley pilaf with lemon rind as a side dish with lamb stew in our restaurant. I think that this pilaf is also great as a side with roasted chicken.

I cover the barley with cold water and soak it overnight. I sauté finely chopped spring onions (scallions) in butter on a medium heat in a medium-size pan. After draining and rinsing the barley in a sieve, I begin stirring it carefully into the butter with a wooden spoon without mashing the barley.

Meanwhile, I boil the chicken stock. After roasting the barley for 5-10 minutes, I add the chicken stock. I add the grated rind of half a lemon, salt and pepper and turn the heat down and leave it cooking with the lid on. Barley absorbs more water than rice does, so it is best to let it cook slowly. After about 20 more minutes of cooking, once the barley is *al dente*, I stir it and let it stand with the lid on. After 10 more minutes, I stir the barley again to make sure the grains do not stick together.

Barley pilaf can be prepared with water when there is no chicken stock. However, the stock balances the lemon nicely, so I recommend using it.
I also like preparing barley pilaf with tomatoes and garlic, dill and spring onions (scallions), and carrots or saffron.

I believe that fragrant herbs go well with barley and bulgur. Like the old women from the south, I like cooking the pilaf with sorrel. Similarly, you can cook these pilafs with finely crushed poppyseeds, chopped spinach or purslane (or watercress).

Whole roast chicken with fresh oregano

1 whole chicken
  (preferably about
  900 g/2 lbs)
Salt
1 bunch of fresh oregano
3 sprigs of rosemary
50 g (1.75 oz/½ stick) butter
Juice of 1 lemon
2 cloves of garlic
Freshly ground black pepper

4 SERVINGS

Wood imparts a great flavour, so we roast chicken in a wood oven in our restaurant. However, if you prefer, you can cook it in the conventional way.

I thoroughly wash and dry the chicken. To get the best results, I salt the chicken the day before. I rub just a bit of salt into the thin parts of the chicken such as the wings, and a lot more on the thicker parts such as the thighs. Lifting the skin of the breast just a little, I insert oregano, rosemary and butter (at room temperature) between the skin and the meat. I wrap the whole chicken with plastic wrap and put it in the refrigerator for a day.

I recommend roasting chicken on a high heat for half an hour, so I preheat the oven to 250°C (485°F/Gas 10) and make sure the fan, if there is one, is running. I rub the chicken with lemon juice and put the squeezed-out lemon rinds inside the chicken. I add whole, unpeeled garlic cloves to the oven dish. (Later, I spread the cooked garlic onto the chicken like paste and eat it with the gravy.) I roast the chicken, breast-side up, for 1 hour, with the first 30 minutes at the pre-set temperature and the second 30 minutes at 180°C (350°F/Gas 4).

It is important that the chicken weighs between 900 g and 1 kg (2-2 lb 4 oz) because larger chickens do not tolerate high heat well. Every 20 minutes, I baste the chicken with the fat and water it releases, making sure not to open the oven door too much.

I serve the chicken steaming hot with a garnish.

If you can't finish the whole chicken, don't worry: you can turn the leftovers into a fantastic chicken sandwich the next day.

Foods that can be served as a side dish with roast chicken
Barley pilaf with lemon, 18
Potato puree with olives, 26
Roast potatoes with rosemary, 30
Crushed potatoes with herbs, 142

Spinach salad with pomegranate

1 kg (2 lb 4 oz) tender
   spinach
1 pomegranate
50 ml (2 fl oz/¼ cup)
   pomegranate syrup
10 g (¼ oz/1½ tsp) honey
100 ml (3.5 fl oz/scant
   ½ cup) olive oil
1 clove of garlic
Sea salt
50 g (1.75 oz) *tulum peyniri* *
   (or emmenthal)
Freshly ground black pepper
50 g (1.75 oz/½ cup)
   chopped almonds

6 SERVINGS

Spinach leaves are firmer than those of lettuce or rocket, so they are more compatible with heavier sauces like pomegranate syrup. It is possible to find spinach throughout the year except in the summer, when the heat gets the better of it. So, it stops growing at the beginning of May, only to reappear at the beginning of September. When making salad with spinach leaves, I keep the roots since delicious things can be made from them. I love eating sautéed spinach roots in olive oil with yoghurt seasoned with garlic.

I start by cutting off the spinach roots and I place the leaves in water. I spoon out the pomegranate seeds into a bowl and, in another bowl, I mix the pomegranate syrup, honey, olive oil, crushed garlic and sea salt into a dressing. If you put this salad dressing in an airtight jar, it will keep in the refrigerator for a day.

I oven-roast the almonds for 10-15 minutes at 120-130°C (250-265°F) and then I crush them using a mortar and pestle.

I cut the *tulum peyniri* * (or emmenthal) into thin strips with a vegetable peeler. I wash and dry the whole spinach leaves and I dress them. I add the almonds and half of the pomegranate and, after tossing again, I put the mixture into a large salad bowl. I add the remaining almonds and pomegranate on top. Finally, I crumble the *tulum peyniri* over the spinach salad and serve.

You can use this pomegranate dressing with herbs and vegetables such as purslane, watercress or garden cress, sorrel and nettles.

* *unpasteurized, soft-ripened, sheep's milk cheese*

Slow-roasted oxtail

1.5 kg (3 lb 5 oz) oxtail
Salt
5 litres (5 quarts) water
2 onions
1 clove of garlic
1 carrot
½ celeriac
Olive oil
2 bay leaves
1 sprig of rosemary
Salt
Freshly ground black pepper
1 bottle Boğazkere
    grape wine (full-bodied,
    tannic red)
100 ml (3.5 fl oz/scant
    ½ cup) boiling water

6 SERVINGS

I soak the meat for 2-4 hours in 5 litres (5 quarts) of water to which I had added a handful of salt to remove the blood.

I quarter the onions without removing their skins and I halve a clove of garlic. I chop the carrot and the celeriac.

I remove the meat from the water and dry it before frying it in a very hot pan until it changes colour. Then I transfer the meat to a large saucepan. I drizzle some olive oil into the pan I used to fry the meat and add the onion, garlic, carrot and celeriac and sauté them for about 10 minutes until they are well browned. Then I put all of the ingredients into a large saucepan and continue sautéing it. First I add the bay leaves, rosemary and salt, and then the wine. To ensure the alcohol in the wine does not catch fire, I add the wine carefully, or I remove the pan from the heat source first. Once the ingredients in the pan have absorbed the wine, I add boiling water and cook the whole thing for about 1.5 hours. Then I remove the cooked meat and strain the remaining gravy before pouring it over the meat.

This is a rich dish, which makes it eminently suitable for winter. Oxtail cooked in this way is also delicious on a bed of pureed aubergine (eggplant).

Roasted rack of lamb and pureed potatoes with olives

For the rack of lamb
Rack of lamb (half a ribcage)
Salt
Freshly ground black pepper
Rosemary

**For the pureed potatoes
with olives**
1 kg (2 lb 4 oz) fresh potatoes
50 g (1.75 oz/½ stick) butter
100 ml (3.5 fl oz/scant
　½ cup) cream
Salt
Freshly ground black pepper
100 g (3.5 oz) black olives
1 bunch of basil

4 SERVINGS

I recommend that for roasting you keep the rack intact rather than separating the individual ribs. There is nothing wrong with a little fat remaining on the meat. Lamb butchered between February and April is less fatty than meat butchered later in the year, so I don't feel the need to remove the fat from them. Having a bit of fat is important to keep the meat from becoming dry and to enhance the flavour. I salt and pepper one side of the ribcage and put it aside.

For the puree

I just cover the potatoes (whole) with cold water in a large saucepan, add a pinch of salt and bring them to the boil on a medium heat. It takes 30-40 minutes for the potatoes to cook, with fresh potatoes cooking fastest. I check with a knife to know when they are done. Once cooked, I drain the potatoes and let them cool. I do not let the potatoes sit in hot water because they will absorb the water. I mash the potatoes after having peeled them while they are still warm. I melt butter in a small bowl and add this, then the cream to the potatoes. After adding salt and black pepper, I cover the bowl with plastic wrap and put it aside. (I don't

refrigerate starchy food that I am going to use the same day because its molecular structure changes as the starch hardens, so when it is reheated, the food loses its freshness and flavour.)

I chop the olives after removing their stones (pits) and I add them and finely chopped basil to the potato and mix it together well.

For the rack

I heat a non-stick pan until it is very hot. Without adding extra fat, I grill both sides of the chops in this pan. I heat the oven to 180°C (350°C/Gas 4), remove the lamb from the pan, and place it on an oven tray and sprinkle chopped rosemary over it. It is enough to roast the cooked lamb chops for 10 minutes.

After removing the ribs from the oven, I cover them with foil for 5-7 minutes to prevent blood showing when you cut them.

Finally, I separate the ribs and serve them with the potato puree mixed with olives.

Fried courgette flowers filled with *lor peyniri*

8 courgette (zucchini)
flowers
250 g (9 oz) *lor peyniri* *
(or ricotta)
1 bunch of basil
100 g (3.5 oz) pine
nuts, roasted
2 cloves of garlic, crushed
Grated rind of 1 orange

for the batter
½ bottle of beer
150 g (5.5 oz/generous 1 cup)
flour
Salt
Hazelnut oil

4 SERVINGS

I buy both varieties of courgette (zucchini) flowers available in Havran market. This indispensible product is picked before sunrise, which is important because courgette (zucchini) flowers close after sunrise and only open ones can be stuffed. Courgette (zucchini) flowers are extremely delicate. They must be used the same day and you should wrap them in a moist paper towel and keep them in the refrigerator until you need them.

I mash *lor peyniri* * (or ricotta), finely chopped basil, pine nuts, crushed garlic and grated orange peel together in a bowl. I fill the courgette (zucchini) flowers with this mixture, beginning with the innermost part of the flowers, and packing down the filling along the way. You can prepare the cheese mixture with different cheeses if you want. Mashed white cheese, Erzincan *tulum peyniri* ** (or fontina), or a mixture of these cheeses and soft cheese works well. Green herbs such as dill, mint and spring onions (scallions) are good to use, too.

I mix some beer, flour and salt in a bowl. I bring the hazelnut oil to a high temperature in a frying pan. After dipping the stuffed flowers into the beer batter, I fry them in the hot oil.

You can serve this dish with strained yoghurt.

* *soft, uncured cheese*
** *unpasteurized, soft-ripened goat's milk cheese local to Erzincan in Anatolia, Turkey*

Rump of lamb marinated in molasses and served with roast potatoes with rosemary

4 SERVINGS

For the rump of lamb
600-800 g (1 lb 5 oz-
    1 lb 12 oz) rump of lamb
50 ml (2 fl oz/¼ cup)
    molasses
2 cloves of garlic
2 sprigs of rosemary
50 ml (2 fl oz/scant ¼ cup)
    olive oil
Salt
Freshly ground black pepper

**For the potatoes
    with rosemary**
½ kg (1 lb 2 oz) fresh
    potatoes
80 g (3 oz/⅓ cup) butter
3 sprigs of rosemary
1 clove of garlic, peeled
Salt
Freshly ground black pepper

Get your butcher to remove the bones from your rump of lamb. The night before I cook it, I rub molasses, crushed garlic, minced rosemary, olive oil, salt and freshly ground black pepper onto the lamb and I put it in a sealed container in the refrigerator overnight. You can use the same marinade for lamb shish kebabs made from rump of lamb.

After washing the potatoes in plenty of water, I place them in an oven dish. I melt butter in a small pan and add the rosemary and garlic. I heat this for 2-3 minutes until the aroma of the rosemary and garlic has permeated the oil, then I pour the mixture over the potatoes. I sprinkle salt and freshly ground black pepper over them and roast them for 40 minutes at 150°C (300°C/Gas 2).

I roast the rump of lamb in a preheated oven at 150°C (300°C/Gas 2) for 2 hours and 20 minutes. I roast the prepared potatoes on the same tray as the lamb, adding them to the tray after 1.5 hours. This makes the potatoes even tastier because they absorb the juices from the lamb.

When I use the same marinade for grilled lamb, I get very good results. I love adding grape molasses to this marinade. You can also add various other kinds of molasses, such as carob molasses. Molasses has its own unique flavour which complements lamb.

Rocket salad with pear and *kelle peyniri*

2 pears
2 bunches of rocket
1 bottle of Öküzgözü
    grape wine (soft,
    fruity red)
100 g (3.5 oz/½ cup)
    granulated sugar
30 g (1 oz/1½ tbsp) honey
150 g (5.5 oz) *kelle peyniri* *
    (or gouda)
10 ml (2 tsp) grape vinegar
Extra-virgin olive oil
Salt
Freshly ground black pepper

4 SERVINGS

I slice pears as I would apples and I cook them with the wine, granulated sugar and honey in a medium-sized pan on a high heat until the pear slices have absorbed the wine. Keep an eye on the pan since the time between the pears absorbing the wine and burning is short. The pears should become dark red, even Bordeaux-like in colour. Once they are ready, I put the pears on a plate.

I crumble the *kelle peyniri* * (or gouda) finely in a food processor, though you may use a normal cheese grater.

I prepare a sauce by adding vinegar, olive oil, salt and black pepper to the wine mixture remaining in the pan.

I rinse the rocket thoroughly and dry it, then toss the crumbled cheese, salad dressing, pear and greens and place the salad in a bowl to serve.

I also like using thinly sliced *kelle peyniri* so it doesn't get lost in the salad. Slices look nice placed on top of the salad.

* hard sheep's milk cheese

White cherry and coriander jam

1 kg (2 lb 4 oz) white
    cherries (or red)
600 g (1 lb 5oz/3 cups)
    granulated sugar
1 vanilla bean
½ a lemon
A pinch of coriander seeds

4 SERVINGS

I pip the cherries, place them in a large pan and pour the sugar over them. I cover the pan and leave it standing 2-3 hours for the cherries to release their juice. Then I add the vanilla bean and boil the cherries on a low heat, using a perforated ladle to skim off any foam as it accumulates. If you want a clearer jam, add a knob of butter. Your jam is ready when drops of it stick to a plate and, once it reaches this stage, add the juice of half a freshly squeezed lemon. Leave the jam to cool a little longer and then remove it from the stove.

If I want whole fruit suspended in the jam, I remove the fruit before the juice thickens and finish cooking the juice until it is ready. Then I return the fruit to the jam and stir it in.

I sprinkle the coriander on the jam and serve.

You can serve this cherry jam as a complement to a cheese platter or mix in *testi peyniri* * (or ricotta as the closest alternative) for a delicious breakfast.

* *a local cheese aged underground in earthenware pot*

WHEN MAKING JAM
Use a wooden spoon.
To keep the jam
free of crystals,
use lemon juice
(not lemon salt).
Put the jam into clean,
dry jars because,
if you leave the jam
in the saucepan,
it will continue
to cook.

Spinach and Ezine cheese pizza

For the dough
35 g (1.2 oz) dry yeast
500 ml (18 fl oz/2¼ cups)
    warm water (60°C/140°F)
1.25 kg (2 lb 12 oz/10 cups)
    flour
30 g (1 oz) salt

Toppings
Olive oil
500 g (1 lb 2 oz) spinach
100 g (3.5 oz) Ezine cheese *
    (or feta or fresh mozzarella)
100 g (3.5 oz) fresh *kaşar
    peyniri* ** (or gruyère)

6-8 SERVINGS

The dough

I dissolve dry yeast in warm water in a large bowl and let it sit for 5 minutes before slowly stirring in 750 g (1 lb 10 oz/generous 5 cups) of the flour and the salt. I fold most of the remaining flour into this watery mixture and continue kneading it, adding more flour until the dough is no longer sticky. I turn the dough out on a floured counter, dust my hands in flour and continue kneading and throwing the dough until it has become smooth, elastic and soft. I put it into a large bowl smeared in olive oil and leave it to prove under plastic wrap in a warm place until it is about twice its original volume (about 3 hours). I divide the dough into four parts and leave them covered with a cloth on a floured work surface for another 20 minutes. Then I roll out the pieces of dough very thinly (about 2 mm/¹⁄₁₆ in), either by hand or, for the less practiced, with a rolling pin.

I heat the oven to 250°C (485°F/Gas 9-10) but, because we use a wood stove, I know the bottom of the oven is always about 180°C (350°F/Gas 4). If you have a gas or electric oven, you can use a stone slab (or even an oven tray) for the same purpose once it is up to temperature.

The topping

After leaving the spinach to soak, I rinse it thoroughly, remove the roots, and pat the leaves dry. I sauté the spinach leaves in a non-stick frying pan with a little oil, spicing it up with salt and freshly ground black pepper just before I remove it.

I put the sautéed spinach on the pizza bases, add the Ezine cheese* (or feta or mozzarella) and *kaşar peyniri* ** (or gruyère) and some olive oil, and put the pizzas in the oven.

The pizza is ready as soon as the cheese has melted and the other ingredients have browned.

* white cheese local to Ezine in Marmara region of Turkey
** unpasteurized, medium-hard sheep's/cow's milk cheese

URLA

HAVRAN

ALAÇATI

URLA

TİRE

MİLAS

MUĞLA

YALIKAVAK

ULA

MARMARİS

DATÇA

BOZBURUN

*H*EADING OUT *of İzmir towards Çeşme is always refreshing. Even thinking of the white horses cresting the waves, the trees lopsided from the prevailing winds, and the wind farms of turning turbines that I'll see makes me fidgety. I love the vineyards, small houses, and to see the bicyclists along the pine-tree-lined road I enter after turning off the İzmir-Çeşme motorway at the Urla sign. At the very end of this road is Urla's modest market, set up at weekends.*

Though small, I can't contain my surprise at the produce I find in Urla market. Samphire, glasswort, rock samphire, hurma *olives, Cretan courgettes (zucchini) with their bright-yellow flowers still attached to their stems and in visual harmony with the stalls, fresh figs, which are precious to the people of İzmir, fresh hazelnuts from Değirmendere,* tarhana *(dried soup mix of flour, cereals, vegetables and yoghurt), pink tomatoes, white tomato peaches that look like they have been stepped on, fennel, wild purslane and more. I like them all so much that I get an overwhelming urge to cook whenever I'm on this peninsula.*

The conversation of the old women in Urla market, who are so sweet and brimming with information, puts you at ease. Moreover, the mottled okra they sell is the best I have ever seen.

You should not miss the afternoon fish auction if you can stay for it. Excitement builds with the size of the crowd around the bowls of fish as the sellers begin raising their prices.

Neither should you miss the small Uzbek market that is occasionally established there.

In every respect, Urla is animated and cheerful. The weather in these parts is pleasant. Even on one of the hottest summer days, I shiver as I drink hot sage tea by the sea. I'd consider wearing my sweater if I had brought it.

One of the specialties of the Urla peninsula is the hurma *olives, which originate on Karaburun, the north-pointing 'thumb' of land that extends from the main peninsula. Hurma olives mature on the branch, so there is no need to salt them. The onshore breezes here cause a mould to form on the olives and this removes their bitterness, making them edible.*

Having come this far, I should also see Karaburun's eponymous main town, so I take an extra hour to go there. This is one of the most westerly points of Turkey. I observe the activities of this tiny town while I'm eating spoonfuls of sakiz (mastic or gum)-flavoured *pudding (see p. 68). Something that Alev Hanım, who I met at the Slow Food Çeşme Convivium, said to me comes to mind: 'This place, which Herodotus is said to have called the window of the world, is the window through which the world breathes.' And it really feels like the people on these coasts are taking deep breaths.*

Dishes capturing the flavours of Urla market
- Lamb stew with cumin seeds and *günbalı*, 42
- Spicy sautéed octopus with fresh oregano, 44
- Toasted *tulum peyniri* and char-grilled aubergine sandwiches, 46
- Minted melon julep, 48
- *Köfte* sandwich and onion rings, 50
- Sour cherry and cinnamon jam, 52
- Hazelnut cake with warm chocolate sauce, 54
- Pine nut and minced meat *börek*, 56
- *Hurma* olives marinated with lavender, 58
- Pink potato crisps, 60

Lamb stew with cumin seeds and *günbalı*

1 kg (2 lb 4 oz) leg of lamb,
  diced
6 large onions
50 ml (2 fl oz/scant ¼ cup)
  olive oil
50 g (1.75 oz/½ stick) butter
3 g (0.1 oz/scant 1 tsp) cumin
  seeds
1 bulb of garlic
30 ml (1 fl oz/2 tbsp)
  günbalı * (or molasses)
2 bay leaves
1 sprig of rosemary
Salt
Freshly ground black pepper
1 litre (34 fl oz/1 quart) water

4 SERVINGS

The best season for lamb is the end of winter and the months of spring, and the least strong-smelling yet tastiest lamb comes from those traditionally raised in Thrace. I prefer buying a whole leg and dicing it myself, but you can ask your butcher to do the dicing. Small lambs have only a thin layer of fat, so make sure that your butcher does not remove it all as the fat adds to the flavour.

I sauté long, thin slices of peeled onion in olive oil and butter in a medium-sized pan. I want them to retain their juices, so I don't put salt in the pan. I add the cumin seeds, which I have crushed in a mortar, and the garlic, which I have peeled. Once the aroma of the cumin is released, I add the lamb and stir. Then I add the *günbalı* * (or molasses) bay leaves, rosemary, salt and freshly ground pepper and stir again before half filling the pan with boiling water. I cover the pan and leave it on a low heat until the meat becomes tender—about 1½ hours. I like using *günbalı*, which is 'cooked' in the sun, because of its soft, rich aroma.

If I want to add more body to this meal, I use red wine instead of water and, if I prepare this as a winter dish, I serve it with *iç pilav* ** and, instead of the cumin, I add a cinnamon stick and a pinch of allspice.

This stew needs to cook for a long time, so the vegetables tend to disintegrate. Even the onions disappear, blending in with the juice of the stew. If you want them to be seen, either use pearl onions or sauté pearl onions in a separate pan with a little water and add them to the stew after they have cooked.

* *molasses made from seedless white grapes dried in the sun*
** *rice cooked with onions, nuts, liver and currants*

Spicy sautéed octopus with fresh oregano

1 octopus, 5 kg (11 lb)

3 litres (101 fl oz/3 quarts)
    water

3 sprigs of parsley

1 orange

5 black peppercorns

1 wine bottle cork

to sauté

50 ml (2 fl oz/scant ¼ cup)
    olive oil

3 g (0.1 oz/1½ tsp) red
    pepper flakes

2 sprigs of fresh oregano

1 clove garlic

Salt

3 bunches of rocket

1 lemon

50 ml (2 fl oz/scant ¼ cup)
    virgin olive oil

4 slices of köy ekmeği *
    (or sour dough)

**Flavours that
complement octopus**

Citrus, red pepper,

fresh oregano,

red wine,

garlic, dill and

spring onions (scallions)

4 SERVINGS

There are two things to keep in mind when buying octopus: it should be over 4 kilos (8 lb 8 oz) and it should be beaten. Octopus shrinks to half its size when cooked. So, if you want it to be tender and meaty, it must be large. Ask your fishmonger if the octopus you have bought has been beaten because the more it has, the more tender it will be.

I boil the whole octopus for 2-2.5 hours in a large pan with water, parsley, the orange (divided into 2), and some black pepper. I throw a wine bottle cork into the pan because I learned from my old chef that this softens the octopus. Once it has become very soft, I turn it out onto a plate.

Cooking octopus

I use a low heat because a high heat toughens octopus meat and makes it harder to cook. Octopus has a strong odour when cooked, so cook it long before you expect your guests to arrive. I like eating the suckers, but you can remove them by skinning the octopus if you prefer.

I separate the octopus's arms from its body and place the body in a non-stick pan, to which I add some olive oil, red pepper flakes, fresh oregano and garlic. Adding a sprinkling of salt, I sauté the octopus for a few more minutes.

I wash and dry the rocket and season it with olive oil and lemon in a separate bowl. I place the octopus on slices of toast and I serve it with rocket.

I cut the still-warm boiled octopus arms into rounds the thickness of a finger and put them on a plate. I drizzle garlic-flavoured olive oil and sprinkle ground red pepper over them, and serve. Alternatively, you can grill (broil) the arms and serve them.

Whenever time allows, I do not use a pressure cooker for octopus. However, in an emergency, it does reduce cooking time to 45-60 minutes.

* village bread, a simple flat bread prepared on a hot
  plate, not baked

Toasted *tulum peyniri* and char-grilled aubergine sandwiches

5 aubergines (eggplant)
Olive oil
8 slices of *köy ekmeği* *
   (or sour dough)
100 g (3.5 oz) Bergama *tulum
   peyniri* ** (or emmenthal)
3 sprigs of fresh oregano
10 g (¼ oz/2 tsp) butter

4 SERVINGS

This toasted sandwich is one of the most popular
luncheon meals at our restaurant.

I choose aubergines (eggplant) that are firm and
dark, and have no green showing on the base. I
char-grill them until they are completely soft and
have acquired a delicious smoky aroma. While still
hot and without wasting any time I peel them and
place them in a bowl. I drizzle some olive oil
over them.

If I let the aubergines (eggplant) stand too long
without peeling them, they will turn dark and
begin to release bitter juices.

This is a double-decker sandwich, so for each
serving I prepare two slices of *köy ekmeği* * (or sour
dough). I spread the aubergine (eggplant) on each
slice, put some thin slices of Bergama *tulum peyniri* **
(or emmenthal) on top, and sprinkle leaves of fresh
oregano over the whole before placing one slice on
top of another to make one sandwich of 2 layers.
Then I put each sandwich in a sandwich toaster and
cook until both sides become hard. Then I spread
butter on them and brown them.

I cut the sandwiches in half, place one half on the
other and serve with pink potatoes as a side dish.

** village bread a simple flat bread prepared on a hot
  plate, not baked*
*** unpasteurized, soft-ripened goat's/sheep's milk cheese
  local to Bergama in İzmir province in Turkey*

Minted melon julep

1 Çeşme melon (or any small,
    sweet, fragrant melon)
1 bunch of fresh mint
50 ml (2 fl oz) vodka
2 gelatine sheets
50 ml (2 fl oz) cold water

6 SERVINGS

I use Çeşme melon if I make this drink in August.
In the early summer, I use small, aromatic sweet
melons as a worthy alternative.

I cut the melon in half and scoop out the seeds
while ensuring that I leave the sweetest flesh,
which is that closest to the seeds. I remove the
melon's skin and cut the melon into pieces, which I
puree in a blender. I pick the mint leaves from their
stems, add the leaves to the melon puree, and blend
them together. I mix the vodka into the resulting
greenish puree.

I put the sheets of gelatine into a bowl and leave
them in cold water to bloom before gradually
adding the gelatine to the puree. I put this mixture
into shot glasses and refrigerate it for 3-4 hours.

You can serve minted melon julep as a refreshing
appetizer, a sorbet between courses, or as a light
after-dinner dessert.

Depending on the season, you can prepare this
julep with strawberries, apricots or peaches, though
you may need to add caster (superfine) sugar to
sweeten it.

Köfte sandwich and onion rings

For the *köfte* sandwich
500 g (1 lb 2 oz) minced beef
500 g (1 lb 2 oz) minced lamb
2 onions
½ bunch of parsley
1 egg
50 g (1.75 oz) breadcrumbs
2 cloves of garlic
Ground red pepper
5 g (0.17 oz/1 tsp) cumin
4 pitas
4 slices of red onion
4 slices of tomato
Rocket
Dijon mustard

For the onion rings
2 large onions
1 (33 cl) bottle of beer
100 g (3.5 oz/scant 1 cup)
    flour
Salt
Tabasco sauce
Hazelnut oil for frying

4 SERVINGS

Köfte (traditional Turkish meatballs)

If you have the butcher mince the meat, make sure that it is only minced once so it has not become too rubbery. I like using a mixture of lamb and beef. You can use only beef if you prefer, but beef is drier than lamb, so the resulting *köfte* may not be tasty. If you are going to grill (broil) the *köfte*, it is better to use slightly fattier meat so that the *köfte* remains moist.

I begin by kneading the minced meat with the chopped onion, finely chopped parsley, egg, breadcrumbs, crushed garlic, red pepper and cumin on a large tray. Then I divide the mixture into 4 and roll it into the shape of *köfte*. The more you knead, the more the ingredients' flavours will permeate one another and the softer the *köfte* will be. Therefore, it is good to knead the *köfte* for at least 20 minutes.

When shaping the *köftes*, remember that they will shrink by one-third when cooking.

Onion rings

I cut the onions into rings. I mix beer and flour in a small bowl and add salt and Tabasco sauce to taste. I dip the onion rings into this mixture and fry them in oil at 190°C (375°F).

Köfte sandwich

I place the *köfte* on a grill and cook it for 2 minutes on each side. I cut the pitas in half and grill (broil) them. Then I spread mustard on one side of the heated pitas (the amount depends on how hot the mustard is), place onion and tomato slices on them, and then add the *köfte*. I add plenty of rocket and close the pita into a sandwich. I serve with onion rings.

You can also grill (broil) the onions and tomatoes.

Sour cherry and cinnamon jam

1 kg (2 lb 4 oz) sour cherries
1 cinnamon stick
600 g (1 lb 5 oz/3 cups)
    granulated sugar
Juice of ½ a lemon

4 SERVINGS

Cherry pips (stones) don't bother me so I prefer
to leave them in, but you may choose to remove
them. The night before serving this dish, I put the
sour cherries, with the cinnamon and sugar, into a
large saucepan and cover it. The next day, when the
cherries have released their juices, I boil them on
a high heat. I add the lemon juice and, after boiling
a little more, I remove them from the heat.

While cooking, I remove the foam as it forms
on the jam and I stir the mixture with a wooden
spoon. The jam is ready when its syrup can form
drops on a plate. I sometimes make the same
recipe with cloves.

If you want the jam to last a long time, put it into
glass jars and close their lids tightly, then turn the
jars upside down in a pan of boiling water, making
sure that the lid is in the water. This will create a
vacuum in the jar. Jars vacuum-sealed like this will
last a long time in the refrigerator.

Hazelnut cake with warm chocolate sauce

250 g (9 oz) bitter chocolate
(70% cocoa)
60 g (2 oz/½ cup) cocoa
125 g (4.4 oz/scant 1 cup)
ground hazelnuts
6 eggs, separated
80 g (2.8 oz/generous ½ cup)
caster (superfine) sugar
185 g (6.5 oz/¾ cup) butter
at room temperature
180 g (6.3 oz/scant 1 cup)
caster (superfine) sugar

For the sauce
400 ml (14 fl oz/1¾ cups)
cream
240 g (8.5 oz) bitter
chocolate (70% cocoa)

MAKES 6 SMALL CAKES

I like buying hazelnuts when they first appear at the beginning of August because of their special flavour at that time.

I break the chocolate into very small pieces and melt them in a metal bowl standing in a pan of boiling water. This method, known as *bain-marie*, allows you to melt the chocolate without burning it with heat applied directly. However, the chocolate pieces need to be as small as possible to melt quickly. I mix cocoa and ground hazelnuts into the melted chocolate and leave it to cool.

Once the chocolate has cooled, I add some egg yolk that I had previously separated and stir it in. It is important that the chocolate is cool or the yolk will cook.

I beat in the caster sugar and the egg whites until they make a thick and frothy mix. For the desired result, you should ensure that there is no yolk whatsoever in the egg white, that the bowl used to beat the egg white is clean and the ambient temperature is not too hot. This process will take about 10 minutes with a whisk. If you opt for an electric beater, begin slowly and gradually increase the speed.

I beat caster (superfine) sugar with the butter and gradually add this to the chocolate mixture. Then I fold in the beaten egg whites into the mixture with a spatula. I do not use a whisk or beaters since so doing lessens the chances of the cake rising properly.

I bake the whole for 45 minutes at 150°C (300°F/ Gas 2) in a pan that has been greased and dusted with flour.

To make the chocolate sauce, I boil the cream and stir in the chocolate pieces with a wooden spoon or spatula to melt the chocolate.

I either drizzle the sauce over the cake hot from the oven and serve it with ice cream, or if I am going to serve it later, I reheat the cake in the oven just before serving, then pour sauce over it. If you store the sauce in the refrigerator, don't forget that you will have to reheat it before serving.

Pine nut and minced meat *börek*

1 onion
Olive oil
500 g (1 lb 2 oz) minced meat
Salt
Freshly ground black pepper
50 g (1.75 oz) pine nuts
2 *yufka* (or filo/phyllo pastry)
80 g (2.8 oz/⅓ cup) yoghurt
90 g (3.2 oz/generous ⅓ cup)
  butter
10 g (¼ oz/2 tsp) red pepper
100 g (3.5 oz/scant ½ cup)
  süzme yoghurt * (or cream
  cheese)

4 SERVINGS

I buy *yufka* (or filo/phyllo pastry) from the market. You can buy it from a *yufka* maker or a bakery. I do not recommend buying *yufka* from supermarkets since they are usually too thick and crumbly.

Pastry filling

I cut onion into small pieces and brown them in olive oil. Once the onions are soft, I add the minced meat and I brown it until it has released its juice. Then I stir it with a wooden spoon and brown further until the juice has been reabsorbed. I add salt and freshly ground black pepper and stir.

I place the pine nuts in a non-stick pan and heat them until they turn pink. Then I add the minced meat.

Rolling the pastry

I put one *yufka* on the other and then quarter them so that I get 8 triangular pieces. I melt 40 g (1.4 oz/ 2 heaped tbsp) of butter and mix it with yoghurt. Then I place a spoonful of minced meat in a strip on the wide end of the triangles of *yufka* and I spread the oil-yoghurt mixture from the strip of minced meat to the tip of the *yufka*. I roll the yukfa into a cylinder and then twist it into a closed spiral. I place the rolls of pastry on an oven tray, brush oil-yoghurt on them and I bake them for 20 minutes at 180°C (350°F/Gas 4).

Preparing the plate

I fry the remaining butter in a small pan, add red pepper and allow it to bubble. I pour it over the *börek* (savoury pastries) and serve with *süzme* yoghurt * (or cream cheese).

* *strained, thickened yoghurt that has been left in a cloth overnight to thicken*

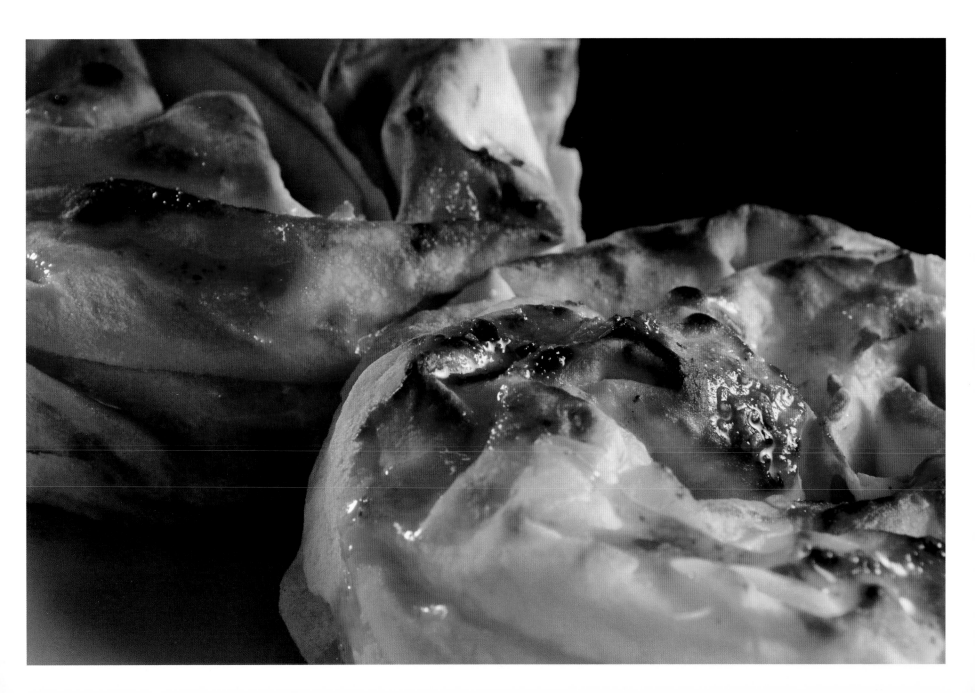

Hurma olives marinated with lavender

100 g (3.5 oz) *kırma*
   (crushed) green olives
100 g (3.5 oz) *hurma* olives
   (or brown/black olives)
100 g (3.5 oz) black olives
100 ml (3.5 fl oz/scant
   ½ cup) extra-virgin
   olive oil
1 orange rind
2 sprigs of oregano
10 g (¼ oz/2 tsp) coriander
   seeds
4 sprigs of fresh lavender

1 JAR

Hurma olives bring a unique flavour to the
Karaburun and Urla area. These olives, cured by
a thin covering of mould rather than by brine,
become edible on the branch (but you can use
brown/black olives instead).

Prior to preparing this recipe, I taste the olives
I have bought. The flavour varies with the
season, the salt content and the firmness of the
olive. If the olives are very salty, I soak them for
a while in water.

I heat half of the olive oil in a small pan, with the
rind of the orange I have peeled (making sure that
I remove the pith), the oregano and the coriander
seeds. I'm careful to keep the oil from becoming too
hot. I add the rest of the olive oil, lavender and the
drained olives to the seasoned olive oil and mix.

You can serve these olives with a drink or at
breakfast. If I'm not going to use the marinated
olives immediately, I replace the orange rind,
oregano and lavender every 2 days. Fresh herbs
make the olives more appetizing.

Pink potato crisps

2 kg (4 lb 8 oz) beetroot
    (beets)
5 litres (5 quarts) water
2 drops of vinegar
2 kg (4 lb 8 oz) Ödemiş
    potatoes (or very small
    Maris Piper potatoes)
Hazelnut oil for frying

4 SERVINGS

I use the least starchy potatoes to ensure I get crispy fried potatoes. Potatoes from the town of Ödemiş are ideal for potato crisps (potato chips), or use very small Maris Piper potatoes instead.

One day before, I peel the beetroot (beets) and boil them in water and vinegar. I remove them from the saucepan and let the water, which is now pink, cool. I cut the potatoes into thin round slices using a potato slicer and put the slices in the pink water to soak overnight in the refrigerator.

The next day, I remove the pink slices from the water and fry them in oil at 190°C (375°F). I place them on a paper towel after frying to absorb excess oil. I salt them and serve.

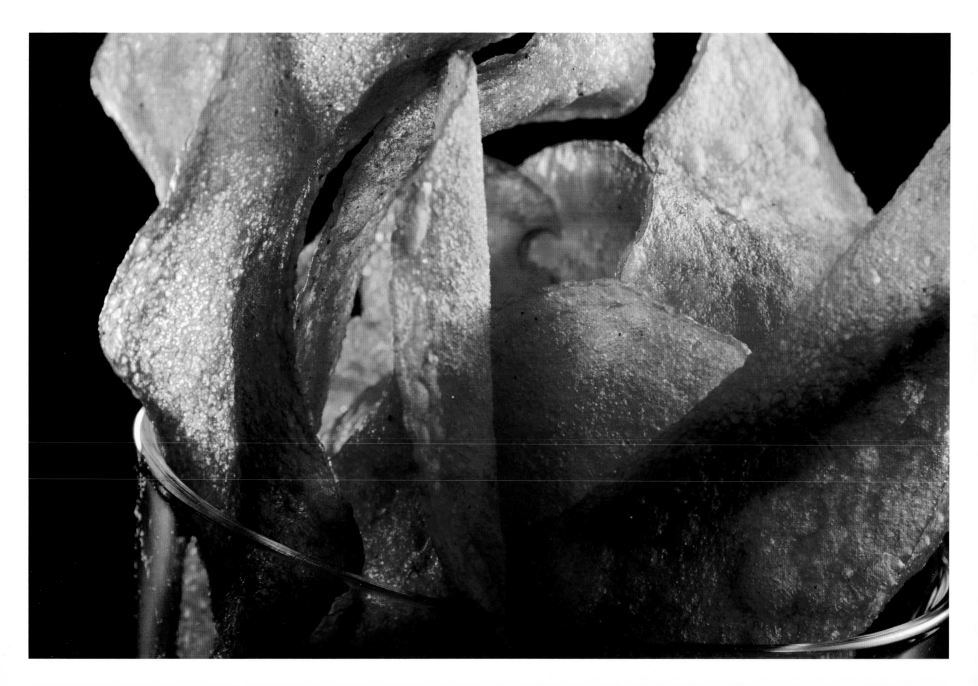

ALAÇATI
ÖDEMİŞ

HAVRAN

ALAÇATI

URLA

TİRE

MİLAS

MUĞLA

YALIKAVAK

ULA

MARMARİS

DATÇA

BOZBURUN

WE LEAVE *the Bozburun Peninsula one Saturday bleary-eyed at four in the morning to arrive at Ödemiş at about eight-thirty, just as the market stallholders are setting up. We start by buying* köy ekmeği *(village bread) made with chickpea yeast from the roadside stalls. Perusing the cheeses, I discover something I have not tried before: a wonderful* çamur peyniri *(a soft, uncured curd cheese). As we walk around the market, I find what we have come for:* hoplatma patates, *small potatoes that are about 1 cm (½ in) in diameter, also called* tohumluk *(seed) potatoes. They are so small that you can just sauté them directly, a favoured local cooking method also called* hoplatma. *After loading kilos of these potatoes into the car, we set off for Alaçatı. The Ödemiş-Torbalı highway passes through Bayındır and there are plant nurseries and flower gardens in every direction as far as the eye can see. This exceedingly pleasant road connects with the motorway, so within an hour we are in Alaçatı.*

As soon as we reach Alaçatı, we knock on the door of Gökçen Abi.[1] Gökçen Abi, whose real name is Gökçen Adar, is an exceptionally knowledgeable food writer. We unwind in his quaint courtyard. Knowing Gökçen Abi enables me to find the best kopanisti peyniri *(fragrant, four-year-old goat's or goat's/sheep's milk cheese local to Çeşme). From there, we visit Gül Fidan Teyze[2] at her stall in Alaçatı market for a chat. We buy a few bunches of samphire to make some of Gökçen Abi's fabulous rock samphire pickles. We fill our shopping bag with* barbunya, *French green beans, and samphire, and we agree to have dinner together.*

Alaçatı has the type of climate that we from the south of Turkey long for: breezy and cool. After watching the windsurfers from the shore and getting some fresh air, we head to Gökçen Abi's for dinner. He is a great storyteller and we listen attentively. As he talks, he conjures up images in my mind of the long, festive dinner tables of his youth. He sings cantatas, prepares exquisite dishes and tells of the local cuisine, providing a captivating evening. We enjoy eating çakıldağı, *a fresh red bean and green bean dish;* sinkonti, *a baked dish of onion, garlic, miniature courgettes (zucchini) and* tulum peyniri *(goat's/sheep's milk cheese);* deniz fasulye *(samphire) with garlic; and* hoplatma patates *sautéed with oregano.*

The next day, I get together with old friends for breakfast under the sakiz *(mastic) trees. Despite having filled myself the night before, the* hurma *olives marinated in olive oil, the honey and butter, black mulberry jam and* lor peyniri *(a soft, uncured cheese), and sliced tomatoes are still very appetizing. In addition to all this, I dip cornbread into grilled* sucuk *(spicy, garlic sausage) and* menemen *(lightly scrambled egg, tomato and green peppers). I can't pull myself away from the wonderful breakfast conversation, so I decide to leave Çeşme's Sunday market until the following week.*

Dishes capturing the flavours of Alaçatı - Ödemiş markets
- Carrot soup with coriander seeds, 66
- Caramelized rice pudding with *sakiz*, 68
- Stewed mussels in olive oil, 70
- Purslane salad with baked beetroot , 72
- Linguine with *kopanisti peyniri* and free-range eggs, 74
- Cauliflower soup and caramelized pear, 76
- Scrambled egg with sautéed courgette and spring onion, 78
- Sole with oregano and *hoplatma patates*, 80

---

1 *Abi* means 'big brother' and is also, here, a respectful expression of closeness to a slightly older male non-relative.
2 *Teyze* means 'aunt' and is also, as here, a respectful expression of closeness to an older female non-relative.

Carrot soup with coriander seeds

1 kg (2 lb 4 oz) carrots
1 onion
10 g (¼ oz/2 tsp) coriander
    seeds
40 g (1.4 oz/2 heaped tbsp)
    butter
50 ml (2 fl oz/scant ¼ cup)
    olive oil
2 litres (68 fl oz/2 quarts)
    water
Salt
Freshly ground black pepper

4 SERVINGS

I peel the carrots, cut them up into five pieces and I chop the onion finely. Then I sauté the onions and coriander seeds in a large saucepan with butter and olive oil on a low heat. Once the aroma of the coriander seeds is released and the onion has sweated, I add water, salt and freshly ground pepper, and I cook the carrots until they are very soft. Then I use a hand blender to puree the vegetables in the saucepan.

I serve the soup with coriander seeds or spring onion (scallions) on top. For a tasty winter soup, you can use curry instead of coriander seeds in the same recipe. If you want to make a creamed version of this soup, stir in 100 ml (3.5 fl oz/scant ½ cup) of fresh cream prior to serving the soup, but don't boil the soup.

Caramelized rice pudding with *sakiz*

35 g (1.25 oz) rice
200 ml (7 fl oz/scant 1 cup)
    water
1 litre (34 fl oz/1 quart) milk
3 g (0.1 oz) *sakiz* (or mastic,
    see right)
A pinch of salt
10 g (¼ oz/2 tsp) rice flour
10 g (¼ oz/2 tsp) starch
50 ml (2 fl oz/¼ cup) water
150 g (5.5 oz/¾ cup)
    granulated sugar
Plain ice cream for topping

4 SERVINGS

I cook the rice in 200 ml (7 fl oz/scant 1 cup) of
water in a small pan on a low heat until the rice
has absorbed the water.

I boil the milk, *sakiz* (or mastic), salt and the cooked
rice in a large pan.

In a small bowl, I prepare a thick mixture of rice
flour, starch and 60 ml (2 fl oz/¼ cup) of water.
I slowly stir this mixture into the milk and rice
and boil for 10 minutes. I add the sugar and boil
for another 2-3 minutes, then I put the mixture
into bowls and leave it to cool off a little.

While the bowls of rice pudding are still warm,
I put them into a preheated oven at 200°C (400°F/
Gas 6) and bake them until the tops brown.

Once cool, I serve with a scoop of plain ice cream
on top. You can infuse the milk with cinnamon,
vanilla or orange peel if you like.

SAKIZ TREE
The *sakiz* (mastic) tree is a short, sturdy,
densely branched tree with greenish flowers
that bloom in April and May and perennial
leaves that remain in winter. It produces
small red fruit. The coagulated sap of this tree,
gum or mastic, is collected from cuts made
in the trunk and branches. The fresh sap appears
green and turns yellow and becomes brittle.
The mastic tree thrives in the Mediterranean
climate and, in Turkey, it is cultivated
around Çeşme, on the Aegean coast.
Greek islanders use *sakiz* to make jam
and a type of *ouzo*.

Stewed mussels in olive oil

75 mussels

2 onions

1 potato

1 celeriac

2 carrots

200 ml (7 fl oz/scant 1 cup)
olive oil

4 cloves of garlic

Salt

20 g (¾ oz/1 heaped tbsp)
granulated sugar

100 ml (3.5 fl oz/scant
½ cup) white wine

1 bay leaf

5 peppercorns

20 g (¾ oz/about 2 tbsp)
flour

200 ml (7 fl oz/scant 1 cup)
water

1 bunch of parsley

4 SERVINGS

WHEN TO BUY MUSSELS

Mussels are at their best outside of their breeding seasons, which are April-May and October-November. The mussel farms in Çeşme do not harvest during these seasons, when the mussels have a soft, jelly-like flesh and carry a risk of poisoning. The seawater they are raised in must be clean, as must the surface to which they adhere, because mussels feed by filtering 20-40 litres (5-10.5 gallons) of water each day and in doing so can concentrate any pollutants.

Only buy mussels that have closed shells, as an open shell indicates that its inhabitant is dead. Do not buy mussels with broken shells. When preparing the mussels, I cut off any carpet-like threads on their shells and clean the shells with a scouring pad or the back of a knife under water. I dice the onion, potato, celeriac and carrots finely; I prefer them small despite the extra effort.

I stir the onions in olive oil in a large pan on low heat. Once they are sweated, I add the carrots, celeriac, potato, garlic, salt and sugar and continue to sauté. I add the wine and cook until it is absorbed. I throw in the bay leaf and black peppercorns. I sprinkle the flour onto the vegetables and cook. Once the dish has absorbed the wine, I add more water and cover the pan. I cook it until the vegetables become soft. When they are almost done, I add the mussels, cover the pan again and wait until the mussel shells have opened. I place the cooling mixture into a bowl and serve with finely minced parsley on top.

This dish makes a delicious entrée or, if served warm, a main course. A mixed seafood stew in olive oil can be made by using fish and other seafood prepared according to this recipe.

I prefer using the small mussels harvested around Çeşme for this dish because they are the perfect size.

Purslane salad with baked beetroot

5 medium-sized beetroot
(beets)
2 cloves of garlic
Salt
100 ml (3.5 fl oz/scant
½ cup) olive oil
2 sprigs of rosemary

200 g (7 oz) Ezine *beyaz
peynir* * (or feta)
100 g (3.5 oz/scant 1 cup)
walnuts
10 g (¼ oz/2 tsp) granulated
sugar
1 kg (2 lb 2 oz) purslane
(wild, if you can find it, or
watercress)

For the sauce
50 ml (2 fl oz/¼ cup)
nar ekşisi (pomegranite
juice reduced to syrup)
1 clove of garlic
Freshly ground black pepper
100 ml (3.5 fl oz/scant
½ cup) extra-virgin
olive oil
Sea salt

4 SERVINGS

I put the beetroot (beets), garlic, salt, olive oil and rosemary on an oven tray, cover it with foil and bake it at 170-180°C (340-350°F/Gas 3-4) for about 90 minutes. Summer beetroot (beets) are small, so they cook easily. If the beetroot (beets) are large, I bake them individually in foil. Once the beetroot (beets) is baked, I peel them and slice them into rounds. I use the olive oil from the baking tray to season them.

I prefer buying aged Ezine *beyaz peynir* *. Cheese (*peynir*) made in March of the preceding year is ideal because the Ezine *beyaz peynir* made then has a greater proportion of sheep's milk, so it is richer in fat. High-fat cheeses age better and are tastier then low-fat ones. I crumble the cheese for this salad.

I bring out the walnuts' flavour by roasting them for 5-7 minutes at 150°C (300°F/Gas 2). While placing the walnuts on the baking tray, I take the opportunity to check each and every walnut again to remove any hidden pieces of shell.

To caramelize the walnuts for this salad, I melt 10 g (¼ oz/2 tsp) granulated sugar in a small pan to make the caramel and then I mix in the baked walnuts. To make the walnuts crispy, use only a small amount of caramel; too much caramel will turn the walnuts into a kind of toffee.

I mix the Ezine *beyaz peynir* and caramelized walnuts with purslane (or watercress) and spread the mixture over the sliced beetroot (beets) on a serving plate. The slightly sour flavour of the purslane highlights that of the beetroot (beets).

I prepare a sauce out of *nar ekşisi* (pomegranite juice reduced to a syrup), crushed garlic, sea salt, freshly ground black pepper and the olive oil. The *nar ekşisi* balances the sweetness of the beetroot (beets).

Preparing the plate

To emphasize the colour of the beetroot (beets), I use a white plate. I serve it with toast.

* *70% sheep's, 20% cow's, 10% goat's milk cheese local to Ezine in Marmara region of Turkey*

Linguine with *kopanisti peyniri* and free-range eggs

3 litres (101 fl oz/3 quarts
water
Salt
1 pack of linguine
50 g (1.75 oz/½ stick) butter
30 ml (1 fl oz/2 tbsp) olive oil
1 clove of garlic
200 g (7 oz) *kopanisti peyniri* *
(or gorgonzola)
4 free-range egg yolks
Sea salt
Freshly ground black pepper
1 bunch of parsley

4 SERVINGS

I bring the water to the boil, add some salt (adding it earlier lengthens the time it takes for water to boil), and throw in the pasta. I don't add oil to the water, but stir the pasta frequently to prevent it from sticking.

For this dish, I want the pasta to be slippery and easy to swallow without using cheese or tomato. I do this by using a little of the cooking water in the preparation of the sauce.

The pasta should be cooked *al dente*. I scoop the pasta out of the water with a ladle, strain it and keep the water for the sauce. I heat the butter, olive oil and a clove of garlic in a pan and stir until the oil is hot enough for the garlic to flavour it, then I add the pasta to the pan and then the cooking water and the crumbled *kopanisti peyniri* * (or gorgonzola). After mixing in freshly ground black pepper and parsley, I apportion the mixture to the plates. I make a well in the middle of the pasta and put an egg yolk in each and mix it in with the pasta to thicken and flavour the dish.

If you prefer a lighter flavour, perhaps because the weather is hot, you can use *beyaz peynir* (or feta) ** instead of *kopanisti peyniri* in this recipe.

* *fragrant, powerful 4-year-old goats' or goats'/sheep's milk cheese local to Çeşme in the Karaburun Peninsula in Turkey*
** *cow's milk cheese*

Cauliflower soup and caramelized pear

1 onion
1 head of cauliflower
500 ml (18 fl oz/2¼ cups)
  cream
300 ml (10 fl oz/1¼ cups)
  milk
1 bay leaf
Salt
Freshly ground black pepper
1 *Deveci* pear (see right, or
  any not too ripe pear)
20 g (¾ oz/1 heaped tbsp)
  granulated sugar
20 g (¾ oz/1 heaped tbsp)
  butter
10 ml (⅓ fl oz/2 tsp)
  pekmez (or molasses; if
  you can find it, *günbalı*)

4 SERVINGS

The creamy texture of cauliflower soup makes it great for winter. I start by peeling an onion and cutting it into pieces without concern for size. I separate the cauliflower florets, put them into a large pan and add the onion, cream, milk, bay leaf, salt and freshly ground black pepper. I simmer this mixture on a low heat for about 20 minutes until the cauliflower is soft. Then I puree the vegetables with a hand blender. I like thick soups, so I serve the soup as it is. However, if you prefer, you can thin the soup with boiling water.

The sweetness of the pear brings out the flavour of the cauliflower. I peel the pear and cut it into cubes, then I sauté it, with butter and sugar, in a non-stick pan until brown. For a stronger flavour, I add a little molasses, preferably *günbalı*, which I stumbled upon in Alaçatı market. It adds a wonderful flavour to the pear.

You can also serve this soup cold after thinning it a little. I prefer serving cold cauliflower soup with smoked seafood or caviar rather than pear.

LÜTFİ DEVECİ AND HIS PEARS
Lütfi Deveci devoted his life to agriculture. Born in the Black Sea city of Samsun in 1912, he chose to live his later years in Alaçatı. In 1960, while returning from hunting, he saw huge pears that greatly impressed him and he decided to trace their origin. Grafting Italian and French pears onto the tree he found, Deveci came up with pears that weighed 1-1.5 kilos (2 lb 4 oz-3 lb 5 oz) each. Deveci pears were found in the village of Ağaköyü, near the city of Bursa, and today a large number of these pears are exported. Deveci pears are also produced around Alaçatı.

Scrambled egg with sautéed courgette and spring onion

4 courgettes (zucchini)
3 spring onions
 (scallions)
1 clove of garlic
30 ml (1 fl oz/2 tbsp) olive oil
4 eggs
2 sprigs of basil
Freshly ground black pepper
Sea salt
A few slices of toast
1 clove of garlic to rub on
 the toast

4 SERVINGS

I select small, dark green courgettes (zucchini). I cut them lengthwise into long thin slices. Then I chop the spring onions (scallions) finely and crush the garlic. I sauté the courgette (zucchini), garlic and spring onion (scallions) in a non-stick pan on a medium heat. I crack the eggs and stir the white and yolk together with a wooden spatula (rather than scramble them with a fork). I tear some basil leaves and sprinkle them on the egg. Then I add black pepper and sea salt.

As soon as the eggs turn white, I remove the pan from the heat. I rub garlic on both sides of some toast and serve it with the egg.

I make the same egg dish with sautéed pumpkin seeds, asparagus, stinging nettles and spinach, depending on the season.

SİNKONTİ
This is Gökçen Adar's recipe.
I lay slices of courgette (zucchini) in an oven dish with onion rings, garlic, *lor peyniri* * (or ricotta), *beyaz peynir* ** (or feta), olive oil and freshly ground black pepper, and bake at 180°C (350°F/ Gas 4) for 15-20 minutes.
Sinkonti is a fantastic summer delight and makes a light meal. I also prepare this dish with pumpkin instead of courgette (zucchini). However, because it releases a lot of water, it is a good idea to add some flour.

* *soft, uncured cheese*
** *cow's milk cheese*

Sole with oregano and *hoplatma patates*

4 sole (300 g/10.5 oz each)
Salt
Freshly ground pepper
Olive oil
20 g (¾ oz/1 heaped tbsp)
  butter
2 sprigs of mountain oregano
  (or oregano)
500 g (1 lb 2 oz) *hoplatma
  patates* (or small potatoes,
  1 cm/½ in diameter)
2 litres (68 fl oz/2 quarts
  water (if normal potatoes
  are used instead
  of *hoplatma patates*)
1 bay leaf
1 handful of salt
50 g (1.75 oz/½ stick) butter
1 handful of parsley

4 SERVINGS

Hoplatma is the local Ödemiş name for new potatoes that are no bigger than 1 cm (½ in) in diameter. These potatoes are so small that they cook as they are sautéed, and during the cooking they are tossed and so they get their name, *hoplatma*, which is derived from the Turkish verb *hoplatmak*, to bounce. Sometimes called seed potatoes, *hoplatma patates* planted in May retain their freshness until August. If they are planted in September, they can be eaten until the end of November or the beginning of December. Because they are very fresh and have thin skins, they do not need peeling or boiling before using.

Sole is fished throughout the winter in the central and southern Aegean. Those caught in open water are ideal since they swim in deep, clean areas. Because sole is thin and delicate, I prefer not to make filets out of it. I gut the fish, wash them well, and dry them with a paper towel. After rubbing them with salt and freshly ground black pepper, I use them whole.

For the sole

I fry each side of the fish in a little olive oil in a non-stick pan, taking 6-8 minutes each side. I put cold butter that I have cut into cubes onto the cooking fish and add fresh oregano onto the melting butter, and I baste the fish with this mixture.

For the *hoplatma patates*

I sauté the potatoes in olive oil and a bay leaf until they are evenly browned. Then I add sea salt, butter and finely chopped parsley.

If I cannot find *hoplatma patates*, I choose small potatoes. After washing the potatoes in plenty of water, I boil them in their skins for 35-40 minutes in 2 litres (68 fl oz/2 quarts) of water with a bay leaf and salt in a large pan. When the potatoes are soft, I melt butter in a separate frying pan, strain the cooked potatoes and transfer them to this second pan. I fry them on a medium heat until they are brown, add finely chopped parsley and serve.

Potatoes boiled with dill are delicious, so you can add a bunch while boiling the potatoes. However, if you use dill in the boiling, add more when sautéing in butter.

Preparing the plate

I place the sole on a large oval plate and serve with potatoes on the side.

TİRE

HAVRAN

ALAÇATI

URLA

TİRE

MİLAS

MUĞLA

YALIKAVAK

ULA

MARMARİS

DATÇA

BOZBURUN

TİRE IS about 20 minutes from Selçuk on a road that passes more peach trees than I have ever seen before. Corn stalks and pomegranate and fig trees line the road to the left and right, and beyond them I am surprised at the number of olive groves toward the hills. In the distance, I see Selçuk Castle, Belevi Mausoleum (built for Lysimachus, one of the Alexander the Great's successors) and ancient stone walls. History and nature are unbelievably and intricately intertwined on the road to Tire.

The market and town are also intricately intertwined, with the stalls crowding all the streets. The herbs, vegetables and fruit are fresh and appealing, with most coming from the highlands of Bayındır village. Cherries, sour cherries and peaches exude a fragrance that even overwhelms the aroma of kebab restaurants. Agog at all this produce, I happen into a street with people selling leek, radish and pepper seedlings. There are also older men and women sitting on stools at the stalls, receiving visitors and chatting.

I ask a gentleman where the felt is sold, and an elderly man who overheard me beckons me to follow him. We pass rope and bell sellers and we stop for tea at a small tea shop and chat with a woman called Hacer, who grows cherries in the hills. After looking about some more, we go by the famous lace-makers, where I am in awe of dozens of stalls and the colourful display of lacework. I buy a few pieces for myself and as gifts.

Then I see a strange sign. A black mulberry and snow sherbet from Bozdoğan for 1 lira (£0.3/US$ 0.5). Snow from Bozdoğan in the middle of July? Indeed—you really ought to taste it. I eat so excitedly that I get brain freeze, but there is an intriguing pleasure in this snowy sherbet in a glass eaten while standing up. The women next to me spooning out the sherbet are from Tire. While chatting about the market, herbs and the area, our conversation turns to the local dairy farms. Tire's villagers are friendly, helpful and smiling people, and just talking to Anatolians gives me a mysterious pleasure in being from this country.

After strolling around the market, I venture up to Kaplan village. Located among chestnut and oak trees on a breezy hill is Lütfü Bey's restaurant, where I eat local dishes and talk at length about seeds indigenous to the area. I top my meal with sweet lor peyniri *(soft, uncured cheese, like ricotta or cottage cheese) covered with mulberry preserves, which has a pleasant taste and can be eaten at any meal, in any season. I fall in love with this village, its smiling people, and its fruits and vegetables, and leave with an enormous smile on my face.*

Dishes capturing the flavours of Tire market
- Ice cream with dates and cognac, 86
- Marinated northern bluefin tuna, 88
- Chicken liver pâté with fig marmalade, 90
- Red snapper with baked cos lettuce, 92
- Sautéed kidney with fresh oregano, 94
- Sautéed chicken *dürüm* with hummus, 96
- Legume soup, 98
- Sweet *lor peyniri* with black mulberry jam, 100
- Sautéed squid with cannellini beans, 102
- Fig tart, 104

Ice cream with dates and cognac

100 g (3.5 oz) dates
100 ml (3.5 fl oz/scant
    ½ cup) cognac
500 g (1 lb 2 oz) vanilla
    ice cream

4 SERVINGS

I put the dates and cognac into an airtight jar. You can keep such a jar in the refrigerator for a long time, but I would not do so for more than a month because I don't want the dates to absorb too much cognac. If I don't have marinated dates available when I need them, I leave some dates in cognac for 2-3 hours at room temperature.

I use vanilla or *kaymaklı* (literally, 'creamy') ice cream, which I let sit at room temperature for 3-5 minutes after I take it from the freezer. Meanwhile, I remove the seeds from the dates, which I cut into small cubes and mix into the ice cream. Then I serve. This goes well with my warm hazelnut cake.

I also make this dish with prunes, dried mulberries or dry figs, but I like the texture of dates the best.

Marinated northern bluefin tuna

1 kg (2 lb 4 oz) tuna
Sea salt
Freshly ground black pepper
2 spring onions (scallions)
Olive oil

4 SERVINGS

BLUEFIN TUNA
A member of the
bonito family,
northern bluefin tuna
is generally found
in the northern Aegean.
It has a firm, red flesh
and those weighing
more than 20 kg (44 lb)
are ideal.

I prefer to eat tuna raw. It is fatty, so marinating the meat from the belly of the fish produces good results.

It is difficult to portion tuna in a home kitchen, so it is best to have this huge fish cut and skinned by a fishmonger. There is a dark section of flesh caused by blood running under the tuna's skin and it becomes visible when filleting the fish. I have this dark part removed and have the fillet divided into 2, giving me 4 large logs of meat.

Buying prepared tuna carries a risk that without the telltale signs of a whole fish, such as bright eyes, it will not be as fresh as you would like. To counter this, tell the fishmonger that you are going to eat it raw and confirm with him that the fish is fresh. Raw fish should be consumed on the same day as it is caught.

Before preparing raw fish, I leave it in the refrigerator for at least 1 hour to give the fish vitality. After removing the fish from the refrigerator, I cut it into very thin slices with a very sharp knife and then I trim the slices to make them round.

At this point, I dust the serving plate with sea salt and freshly ground black pepper and place the fish slices on top. Once the entire platter has been covered with the fish, I add more sea salt and freshly ground black pepper, drizzle a goodly amount of olive oil over it, and sprinkle finely chopped spring onion (scallions) on top. Then it is ready to serve.

I think lemon is more appropriate for fish with white meat rather than for tuna, but you can try different seasonings as your palate desires. Black olives, red onions and a sparing amount of fresh ginger go well with tuna.

Chicken liver pâté with fig marmalade

For the pâté

1 kg (2 lb 4 oz) chicken liver
1 onion
30 ml (1 fl oz/2 tbsp) olive oil
40 g (1.4 oz/2 heaped tbsp)
    butter
1 sprig of fresh oregano
50 ml (2 fl oz/¼ cup) cognac
Salt
1 bay leaf
Freshly ground black pepper
50 ml (2 fl oz/¼ cup) cream

30 g (1 oz/2 tbsp) butter
Sage leaves (optional)

For the marmalade

200 g (7 oz) dry figs
¼ onion
30 ml (1 fl oz/2 tbsp) vinegar
20 g (¾ oz/1 heaped tbsp)
    granulated sugar
10 ml (⅓ fl oz/2 tsp)
    olive oil

8 RAMEKINS SERVES 16

Chicken liver is generally sold attached to hearts, so first I separate them. If I see any membranes, I also remove them.

I chop the onion finely. When making pâté, the onions are also pureed, but the smaller you cut vegetables, the better the flavour.

I heat a large frying pan at a high temperature and drizzle oil on to it and sauté the liver. I add half of the butter and the fresh oregano and brown the liver for about 3-5 minutes, until it is the colour of pomegranates. Don't fill the pan with too much liver because it will boil rather than fry. So, if needs be, I sauté the liver in 2 groups. Also, I don't overcook chicken liver. Inside it should remain pink and moist. At this point, I pour cognac on the liver while it is still in the pan. Cognac is highly flammable and it will ignite when it hits a very hot pan. To prevent this, remove the pan from the heat source, then add the cognac and return the pan to the stove. It takes about 30 seconds for the alcohol to evaporate; during this time, stand back from the pan. Once the cognac is absorbed, you can add the salt. I do not add salt at the start of sautéing because the salt will draw out the juice of the liver and prevent it frpm frying.

I stir the onion and part of the remaining butter in another pan on low heat. I flavour it with bay leaf and freshly ground black pepper. Then I place the onion and the liver into a deep bowl, add cream and puree the whole with a handheld blender. I taste the pâté and add additional salt and pepper if needed.

I melt 30 g (1 oz/2 tbsp) of butter in a small pan.

I divide the pâté into small white porcelain bowls, place a sage leaf on top of each, and put a very thin layer of melted butter over them. This butter helps the pâté stay fresh longer. You can use glass bowls instead of porcelain ones if you wish.

For the fig marmalade

I cut the dry figs into ½-cm (¼-in)-sized cubes. I sauté them for 5 minutes in a pan of melted butter, along with the onion, making sure they do not become dark. After adding vinegar and sugar, I mix all of the ingredients together and cook for another 10 minutes. I remove the pan from the stove and let the mixture cook. Afterwards, I put it in the refrigerator in a glass jar.

Preparing the plates

I serve the liver pâté with toast and fig marmalade.

Red snapper with baked cos lettuce

4 red snapper fillets
  (total 2 kg/4 lb 8 oz)
Salt
Freshly ground black pepper
Olive oil
100 ml (3.5 fl oz/scant
  ½ cup) white wine
1 bay leaf

2 leaves of cos lettuce
Salt
Freshly ground black pepper
Olive oil

8 SERVINGS

RED SNAPPER
Red snapper are large;
the smallest being 1.5-2 kg (3 lb 5 oz-4 lb 8 oz).
For this recipe, buy either a large fish to make
four fillets or one large fillet from a 2 kg (4 lb 8 oz)
fish. Red snapper is generally found in the
Aegean and the Mediterranean. Its firm,
white meat makes it a delicious fish.
It is not very fatty so care is needed
to cook it without it becoming dry.

For the red snapper

Have your fishmonger gut the fish. What's more,
if you think you might have difficulty filleting
this large fish, ask him to do that for you also,
making sure he leaves the skin on. To fillet this
fish yourself, insert a knife under the head until
you reach the bone. Then separate the flesh
from the bone by running the knife parallel to
the work surface.

I start by seasoning the fillets with salt and black
pepper. I put them into a pan preheated to a
medium temperature and with a little olive oil.
After 3-4 minutes, I turn the fillets over and I cook

them for another 1-2 minutes. I add white wine
and a bay leaf and simmer the fish for another
3-5 minutes. The precise cooking time depends
on the thickness of the fish. What is important
is to remove the fish from the pan as soon as it as
cooked so that it doesn't get tough. I keep the sauce.

For the cos lettuce

I heat the oven to 150°C (300°F/Gas 2). I place the
lettuce leaves in a greased oven dish, with salt,
black pepper and a little olive oil on top. I bake
the lettuce for 15-20 minutes, until it has softened.

Preparing the plate

I serve by putting half of the lettuce on top
of the fillet and drizzle the white wine sauce over
it. This recipe makes a very light meal. If I want to
enhance the flavour and richness of this recipe, I
add 20 g (¾ oz/1 heaped tbsp) of cold, diced butter
to the white wine sauce.

I prefer baking or sautéing to grilling red snapper
because its meat can easily become dry if barbecued.

Sautéed kidney with fresh oregano

500 g (1 lb 2 oz) kidneys
Salt
50 ml (2 fl oz/scant ¼ cup)
    olive oil
1 sprig of fresh oregano
10 g (¼ oz/2 tsp) freshly
    ground Albanian pepper
    (or red pepper flakes)
50 g (1.75 oz/½ stick) butter

4 SERVINGS

I prefer to leave the fat on the kidneys, though removing it is a healthier option. I cut the whole kidneys down the middle into 2. After salting the kidneys well, I begin sautéing them in olive oil.

I add fresh oregano and Albanian pepper (or red pepper flakes) once both sides of the kidneys have browned and continue frying. When the insides of the kidneys have turned a light pink, I add butter to the kidneys in the pan.

I serve with toasted bread.

You can make this dish with diced kidneys if you prefer.

Sautéed chicken *dürüm* with hummus

500 g (1 lb 2 oz) chicken
   breast
30 ml (1 fl oz/2 tbsp)
   molasses
2 cloves of garlic
Salt
Freshly ground black pepper

For the hummus
250 g (9 oz) dried chickpeas
1 litre (34 fl oz/1 quart) water
200 g (9 oz) tahini
2 cloves of garlic
½ a lemon
Cumin
Powdered red pepper
Olive oil
Salt

1 bunch of rocket
4 thin *lavaş* (or unleavened
   bread)

4 SERVINGS

For the chicken

Take 2 finger-sized pieces of chicken breast
and marinate them in molasses, crushed garlic,
salt and freshly ground black pepper, either for
15-20 minutes at room temperature or for
3-4 hours in the refrigerator.

For the hummus

I boil the chickpeas that I had left soaking
overnight in 1 litre (34 fl oz/1 quart) of water until
soft. I do not add salt while boiling because that
makes legumes tough. While the chickpeas are still
warm, I mix them well with the tahini, garlic and
lemon juice. I then puree the mixture in a blender
at high speed. I add cumin, red pepper, olive oil and
salt to taste.

For the *dürüm* (flatbread wraps)

I brown the marinated chicken in a very hot Teflon
pan, turning the pieces while doing so. Then I heat
the *lavaş* (or unleavened bread), spread 2 large
spoons of hummus on them, and add the chicken,
sliced diagonally, and rocket. I cut the *dürüms* in
half and serve.

Legume soup

For the vegetable stock
1 carrot
1 onion
1 celeriac
1 leek
1 clove
Salt
Bay leaf

100 g (3.5 oz) cooked
   chickpeas
100 g (3.5 oz) cooked beans
100 g (3.5 oz) fresh peas
100 g (3.5 oz) pinto beans
1 clove of garlic

6-8 SERVINGS

To make the vegetable stock, I peal those vegetables that need it and then chop all the vegetables into pieces without much regard to the size. I cook them for 1.5 hours in 4 litres (4 quarts) of water with a clove, some salt and a bay leaf, and then I strain the vegetables and retain the stock. I add boiled legumes, peas and a clove of garlic and cook for another 20 minutes.

I remove the garlic before serving.

You can also make this recipe using chicken stock.

Sweet *lor peyniri* with black mulberry jam

1 kg (2 lb 4 oz) black
    mulberries
100 g (3.5 oz/½ cup) sugar
Juice of ½ a lemon
200 g (7 oz/scant 1 cup)
    sweet *lor peyniri* *
    (or ricotta)

4 SERVINGS

I put the mulberries and sugar into a pan and
let the mixture stand for an hour. Then I simmer
the fruit on a low heat for half an hour. I remove
the cooked fruit from the juice and continue
cooking the juice for another 15-20 minutes until
it has become quite thick.

I squeeze the juice of half a lemon into the pan and
remove it from the stove. Then I put the fruit back
into the juice and set it aside to cool. I like putting
these preserves over sweet *lor peyniri* * (or ricotta)
for breakfast or as a dessert.

* *soft, uncured cheese*

Sautéed squid with cannellini beans

2 squid tubes
1 bottle mineral water
100 g (3.5 oz) cannellini
    beans
1 bay leaf
Black peppercorns
Olive oil
2 sprigs of fresh oregano
10 g (¼ oz/2 tsp) powdered
    red pepper
¼ bunch of parsley
1 clove of garlic
20 g (¾ oz/1 heaped tbsp)
    butter
Salt

4 SERVINGS

I clean the squid tubes as in the stuffed grilled
squid recipe (see p. 240). After washing it well, I
open one end of the tube-shaped squid and make
a rectangle out of it. Then I score the squid with a
knife at intervals of 1 cm (½ in), vertically and then
horizontally. After this, I let the squid sit in mineral
water for an hour at room temperature.

I boil the beans with the bay leaf and black
peppercorns, but no salt, until they are soft.

I heat a large Teflon pan to a high temperature and
then add some olive oil and I sauté the squid, which
I have already cut into finger-thick slices. Once the
squid begins to change colour, I add fresh oregano,
powered red pepper, finely minced parsley and
a peeled clove of garlic, along with butter. After
sautéing the mixture for 2-3 minutes, I serve it.
Squid should be sautéed at high temperatures; at
low temperatures it becomes tough and chewy.

I prefer serving this dish as an appetizer. If you
don't add butter, you can mix the squid into salad.

Fig tart

150 g (5.5 oz/⅔ cup) butter
250 g (9 oz/2 cups) flour
60 g (2 oz/generous
    ¼ cup) caster sugar
    (superfine sugar)
1 egg
1 pinch of salt

250 ml (8.5 fl oz/1 cup) milk
60 g (2 oz/generous ¼ cup)
    sugar
Vanilla bean (optional)
50 g (1.75 oz/scant ½ cup)
    cornflour (cornstarch)
2 egg yolks

8 fresh figs

⌇

FIGS
Figs are generally
available from
the end of July
until the end of
September.
First green figs ripen
and then those on
black fig trees.
The green *bardacık* figs
sold in Tire market are
the best I have ever
eaten. When buying figs,
I make sure that
they are not too soft.

⌇

6-8 SERVINGS

I cut the cold butter into cubes and add them to flour and salt in a food processor to mix to a breadcrumb consistency. (You can do this by hand if you wish.) I then knead the mixture on a work surface, make a hole in the middle, add the sugar and the egg, and then lightly knead again. I form the mixture into a ball, wrap it in cling film and let it sit in the refrigerator for half an hour. Unlike bread dough, kneading tart dough too much will spoil its texture. I knead the mixture only to the point where the ingredients have just begun to hold together.

I remove the dough from the refrigerator and shape it into a thick cylinder. Then I cut off ½-cm (¼-in)-thick circular slices, shape them by hand and lay them on an oven tray covered with greaseproof paper. Using a fork, I pierce the dough to keep it from lifting. I bake the pastries in an oven preheated to 180°C (350°F/Gas 4) for about 10 minutes, until they have become golden brown. I remove them from the oven to cool.

Reserving half a glass, I put the milk into a pan with half the sugar and the vanilla bean and boil. I mix the milk I have reserved with the cornflour (cornstarch).

I fold the other half of the sugar into the egg yolks and I blend the egg and milk-starch mixtures together. I gradually add it to the milk mixture on the stove and continue whisking it. It is necessary to whisk rapidly to keep it from becoming lumpy. Once it has a consistency that is slightly less thick than that of pudding, I remove it from the stove and keep stirring. This mixture can be kept for up to 2 days in the refrigerator.

I put the mixture into a pastry bag and squeeze it over the cooled tart crusts. I cut the fresh figs into slices and place them on top and then serve.

I like using seasonal fresh fruit such as raspberries, mulberries, grapes and apricots.

MİLAS

İLAS IS a large district in Muğla province. It has more villages than any other in Turkey and it encloses a wide valley stretching from Lake Bafa in the north to Bodrum in the south. Like the district, the market in the eponymous provincial capital is sprawling and of many parts. Milas market, held every Tuesday, draws stallholders from a wide area, selling everything from a few bottles of sheep's milk and a bit of cheese to sacks of beans, strained yoghurt, hundreds of varieties of herbs and handmade carpets and potted flowers. One word sums up this market neatly: 'variety'.

I leave home at sunrise to get to the market in good time. Approaching from Yatağan, the first I see of Milas is a city swathed in a thin mist. After passing groves of olive trees, I plunge into the market. My feet draw me to deliciously fragrant, herb-filled crêpes. I buy one and eat it with delight. I fill my cloth bag with a kilo (2 lb 4 oz) of pine mushrooms, which are begging to be sautéed with tiny onions. I also buy the deepest-orange pumpkin I can find to caramelize.

While Milas market is a pleasure in all seasons, it has a special beauty in the autumn and winter. Browsing the stalls—brimming with herbs, mushrooms, quinces, pomegranates and walnuts at this time—is a large part of its attraction, which is deepened by a strange, inexplicable melancholy that casts a spell over the market. Though the market's produce is varied, the stalls are widely spaced, replacing vibrancy with solitude.

AEGEAN FLAVOURS

It would be a sin to travel as far as Bodrum without visiting Milas market. I recommend going there by boat across the gulf from Bodrum at the end of September or the beginning of October, when the sea is like a millpond. While in Gökova, take the opportunity to buy fish from the small boats and to see the market, chat with the sellers tending colourful stalls, to learn the ins and outs of mushroom picking and then prepare scrumptious meals from the fresh ingredients. Make the journey worthwhile by baking the head of a large grouper and eating its cheeks: the tastiest part of the fish.

Dishes capturing the flavours of Milas market

- Whiting with olive oil and fennel, 110
- Grilled chicken with green olive sauce and sorrel salad, 112
- Baked pumpkin with vanilla sauce, 116
- Pizza with red onion, tomatoes, olives, fresh oregano and *köy peyniri*, 118
- Sautéed monkfish with green apple and fennel salad, 120
- *Lor peyniri* and mallow *börek*, 122
- Purslane salad with tahini and hazelnuts, 124
- Char-grilled vegetable salad with basil, 126
- Mussels steamed in *rakı*, 128
- Dusky grouper baked in milk, 130

Whiting with olive oil and fennel

1 fennel bulb
1 onion
10 spring onions
   (scallions)
2 cloves of garlic
200 ml (7 fl oz/scant 1 cup)
   olive oil
30 g (1 oz) flour (as desired)
150 ml (5 fl oz/generous
   ½ cup) white wine
10 g (¼ oz/2 tsp) granulated
   sugar
Sea salt
Freshly ground black pepper
150 ml (5 fl oz/generous
   ½ cup) water
1 kg (2 lb 4 oz) whiting
1 bunch of dill
½ bunch of parsley
1 bunch of fresh mint

4 SERVINGS

While fennel bulb can be found year round in large cities, local markets only have it in winter and spring, and spring is usually the best time because the fennel is fresh but has not yet gone to seed.

I chop 1 cm (½ in) off the bottom of the fennel bulb to remove its hard, inedible base. Then I cut the main body of the fennel down the middle and slice it thinly. I dice the onion and cut the spring onions (scallions) lengthwise. I cut the garlic cloves into two. I sauté all of the ingredients in olive oil in a medium-sized pan on medium heat for 10 minutes. I make sure that the onions don't change colour very much. If you want the consistency to be watery, you can leave out the flour, but I prefer to use a little. I add white wine and let it reduce for 2-3 minutes. After adding sugar, salt, freshly ground black pepper and water, I let it simmer for 15-20 minutes.

I cut the fish lengthwise into 3 cm (1¼ in) strips and add them to the simmering mixture. After cooking for 5 minutes, I turn off the heat and I let the pan cool without removing the lid.

I finely chop the dill, parsley and fresh mint and add these to the cooled fish dish, making sure I don't crush the fish.

You can also make this dish with whiting, mackerel and gurnard.

Fennel is a pungent root vegetable. If the aroma from the fennel is too great, you can also make this dish without it. You can use fresh celery, plenty of spring onion (scallion), or red onion instead.

Grilled chicken with green olive sauce and sorrel salad

2 whole chickens
 (plucked and drawn,
 though chicken thighs
 on the bone can
 also be used)
30 g (1 oz) yoghurt
10 g (¼ oz/2 tsp) tomato
 paste
A pinch of red pepper
2 cloves of garlic
2 sprigs of rosemary
50 ml (2 fl oz/scant ¼ cup)
 olive oil
Salt

For the green olive sauce
150 g (5.5 oz) green olives
1 shallot
A few drops of vinegar
2 sprigs of fresh oregano
2 sprigs of parsley
½ grated lemon rind
Extra-virgin olive oil

For the salad
½ an onion (to clean
 the grate of the grill)
1 bunch of sorrel
1 lemon
Sea salt

4 SERVINGS

To bone the chicken

A whole chicken is fatter and tastier than chicken pieces, so I prefer to buy one of these and bone it myself. If this is too difficult a proposition, you can use chicken thighs.

I lay the chicken on its back on a cutting board with its legs facing me. Taking a sharp knife, I cut alongside the cartilage. Then I cut the breast meat from the ribcage and pull the meat back. I turn the chicken over and I severe the thigh from the main body of the chicken, leaving it attached to the breast meat. The thigh bones are still in the thighs, so I make an incision along the length of the leg bones on the inside of the legs and I separate the meat from the bones with the knife.

We remove crates full of bones everyday in our restaurant, so this process seems easy to us. In time, you, too, can become adept at this. Alternatively, if you prefer, you can buy thighs and remove the bones without having to work so hard. The choice is yours.

I place the 4 pieces of boneless chicken (with their skin on) into a dish. In a separate bowl, I mix yoghurt, tomato paste, red pepper, crushed garlic, rosemary, olive oil and salt thoroughly with a fork and then pour it over the chicken. I seal the dish with plastic wrap and leave the chicken to marinate for a few hours in the refrigerator. However, if you are in a hurry, you can let it stand for 15-20 minutes at room temperature and then use it.

For the green olive sauce

I remove the seeds (pits) from of the olives and peel the shallot and quarter it. I blend the olives, shallot, a few drops of vinegar, fresh oregano leaves and parsley. I add grated lemon rind and a bit of olive oil to this mixture and bring it to the consistency of a sauce.

>>

Grilled chicken with green olive sauce and sorrel salad (continued)

The grilling (broiling)

I light the grill (or preheat the broiler) and wait for it to become glowing embers (medium hot). I clean the grill with half an onion spiked on a fork. I place the marinated chicken on the grill (under the broiler). If the grill is not hot enough, the chicken will stick to it, but make sure the chicken is not too close to the embers or else the dripping fat will catch fire.

For the sorrel salad

I love sorrel because of its characteristic tartness. You can also use cress, rocket, purslane or tender spinach for this salad. I soak the sorrel leaves in cold water, and rinse and drain them in a sieve or, preferably, a salad drier. Dry leaves make the best salad because wet leaves prevent the dressing from adhering and they wither quickly.

I mix a pinch of salt with the lemon juice and slowly add olive oil. At this point, you can also add mustard, garlic, parsley or whatever comes to mind. So as not to compromise the taste of the green olives, I keep the salad dressing as simple as possible.

Preparing the plate

I put the crispy chicken onto a plate and drizzle the olive dressing over the top and serve the sorrel salad on the side.

Flavours that complement chicken

Basil, bay, butter, carrot, garlic, lemon, olive, freshly ground black pepper, rosemary, tomato, wine, yoghurt, mustard, honey and rice

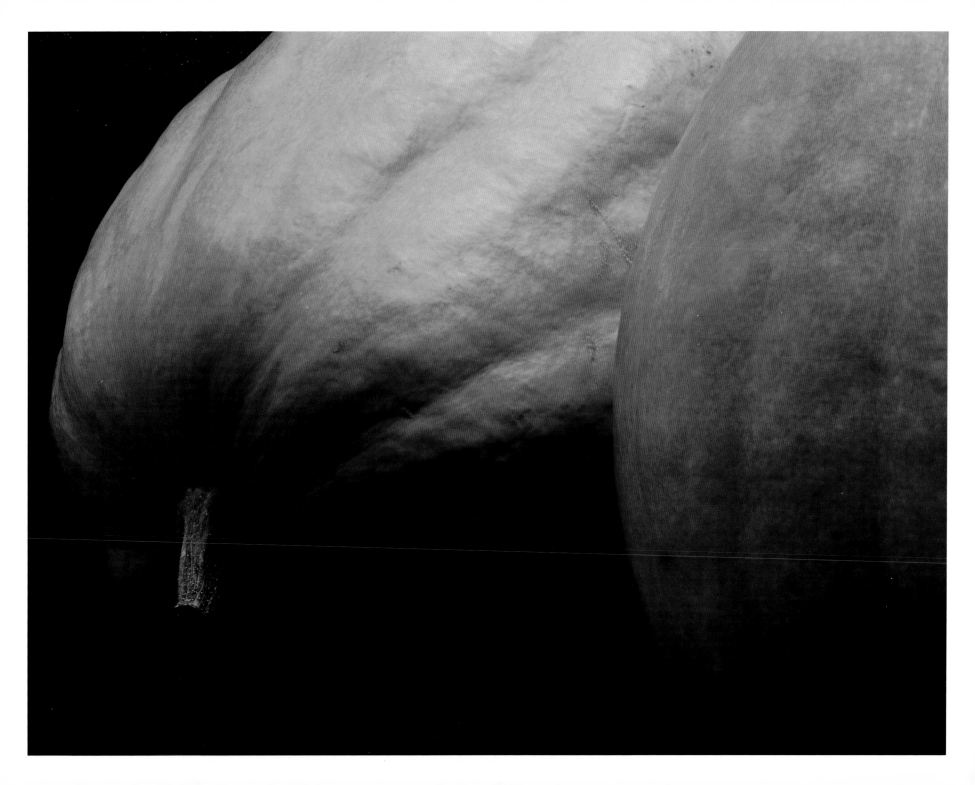

Baked pumpkin with vanilla sauce

1 kg (2 lb 4 oz) pumpkin
500g (1 lb 2 oz/2½ cups)
    granulated sugar
2 cloves
1 cinnamon stick
250 ml (8.5 fl oz/1 cup) water

For the vanilla sauce
1 vanilla bean
250 ml (8.5 fl oz/1 cup) milk
3 egg yolks
150 g (5.5 oz/1¼ cup) sugar

4 SERVINGS

For the pumpkin

We use the whole pumpkin to make this dessert, peeling and slicing it ourselves rather than buying pumpkin slices. I cut large slices, arrange them on a baking tray and sprinkle them with sugar. I boil the cloves and cinnamon with the water in a small pan and pour the whole concoction, including the pieces of cloves and cinnamon, onto the pumpkin, cover it with foil and slip it into an oven at 180-200°C (350-400°F/Gas 4-6) for 1 hour. Then I turn the pumpkin slices over and return the uncovered tray to the oven for another 20 minutes to caramelize the top. Finally, I remove the tray from the oven and let it cool.

For the vanilla sauce

I cut the vanilla bean lengthwise and remove the seeds with a knife. Then I put the bean and the seeds into the milk and simmer it for 20 minutes.

I beat the egg yolks and sugar in a large bowl for 8-10 minutes until they become thick. Slowly adding the milk and stirring constantly, I cook the mixture on a very low heat for 1-2 minutes. (Cooking on a high heat of for too long will result in an omelette.) To ensure a smooth vanilla sauce, I stir it rapidly and remove it from the heat if it gets too hot. After cooking the sauce, I store it in the refrigerator.

Preparing the plate

I place a piece of pumpkin in the middle of a plate, pour vanilla sauce over it and serve.

Flavours that complement pumpkin

Cheese, cinnamon, cloves, cream, curry, garlic, ginger, sage, sugar and vanilla

Pizza with red onion, tomatoes, olives, fresh oregano and *köy peyniri*

For the dough
35 g (1.2 oz) dry yeast
500 ml (16 fl oz/2 cups)
    warm water (60°C/140°F)
1.25 kg (2 lb 12 oz/10 cups)
    flour
30 g (1 oz) salt

For the topping
1 red onion
20 black olives
2 tomatoes
1 handful of fresh oregano
120 g (4 oz) fresh *köy peyniri* *
    (or try fresh buffalo
    mozzarella)
Olive oil

8 SERVINGS

To make the dough, see the recipe for spinach pizza, p. 36

I slice the red onion into very thin rings and I remove the seeds from the black olives. I either slice the tomatoes thinly or quarter them. I strip the leaves from the oregano stems and I cut the *köy peyniri* * (or fresh buffalo mozzarella) into 3-cm (1¼-in)-thick slices.

I roll out the dough and cover it with cheese and then the red onion, tomatoes, oregano and black olives. I drizzle a little olive oil over the top and bake it until the cheese has melted and the other ingredients have browned. The pizza is now ready.

If you do not have a pizza stone, you can also use a heated oven tray.

* village cheese, a fresh, semi-soft and not very salty cheese from cow's/goat's milk

Sautéed monkfish with green apple and fennel salad

1 kg (2 lb 4 oz) monkfish
Sea salt
30 g (1 oz) mustard
Olive oil
1 clove of garlic
1 fennel bulb
1 green apple
1 orange
1 lemon
Salt
Freshly ground pepper
Extra-virgin olive oil

4-6 SERVINGS

MONKFISH

Monkfish are ugly. Their heads are much larger than the rest of their bodies. They have white meat that, although it has a heavy smell while raw, is firm and tasty when cooked. Monkfish are found in the Marmara, Aegean and Mediterranean seas between September and February. Very small and very large monkfish have too much waste, so I prefer medium-sized ones. Though monkfish may seem cheaper than other fish available around Turkey, the waste makes it about 20% more expensive. Its meat has an intense flavour, so I prefer to sauté, grill or broil it or to make shish kebab from it. A pungent white wine or a light red wine complements the flavour of this fish.

Flavours that complement monkfish

Basil, garlic, lemon, butter, bay, red wine and rosemary

For the monkfish

I have the fishmonger remove the fish's head and skin. I remove the thick bone that runs down the middle of the fish and I cut the fish into 2 parts. After salting and peppering it, I rub mustard and olive oil into it and I leave it to sit in the refrigerator for half an hour.

Preparing the fennel salad

I cut 1 cm (½ in) off the bottom of the fennel because that part is too hard to eat. I divide the fennel in 2 and slice it finely. I cut the green apple into 2, without peeling it and, after coring it, I slice it thinly.

Using a peeler, I remove strips from the orange and lemon rinds. I then cut the strips lengthwise so it is like string. I squeeze the juice out of the orange and lemon and then mix olive oil with it to make a sauce.

For the fish

I heat the oven to 180°C (350°F/Gas 4). I put the fish onto a very hot medium-sized non-stick pan and sauté it until it is brown on all sides. I peel the garlic and cut it into two down the middle and add it and some olive oil to the pan. I leave the fish in the pan for 1 minute before I transfer it to an oven dish and bake it for 5-8 minutes in the preheated oven.

Preparing the plate

Taking the fish out of the oven, I cut it into thin round slices 1 cm (½ in) thick. I mix the fennel and green apple, lemon sauce and orange and lemon rinds. I spread the fennel salad onto a long plate and lay the fish pieces on it.

Lor peyniri and mallow *börek*

1 kg (2 lb 4 oz) mallow
　　(or nettles, turnip greens
　　or spinich)
1 bunch of spring onions
　　(scallions)
100 g (3.5 oz) pine nuts
200 g (7 oz) sweet *lor peyniri* *
　　(or ricotta)
Salt
Freshly ground black pepper
3 *yufka* (or filo/phyllo pastry)
Hazelnut oil for frying

24 PIECES

Instead of mallow, you can use nettles, turnip greens or spinach for this *börek* (savoury pasty).

For the *börek*

I like to soak leafy vegetables in water with a drop of vinegar before washing them so that any bugs will detach. I then thoroughly rinse the leaves and dry them in a sieve.

I sauté the mallow in small quantities in a large, hot skillet with a little olive oil. If the skillet is not hot enough or you sauté them in large quantities, the leaves will release water and boil. After sautéing the leaves, I put them into a sieve to let any water remaining in the leaves to drain. I add finely chopped spring onions (scallions) to the pan and cook them for a few minutes. Then I put the leaves on a plate, mix them with the spring onions (scallions) and leave it to cool.

I brown the pine nuts in a non-stick pan for 2-3 minutes. Then I add them and *lor peyniri* * (or ricotta) to the pan that I used to cook the mallow and the spring onion (scallions) and mix them together and I add salt and freshly ground pepper. I use sweet rather than sour *lor peyniri* for the pastry.

If you want a more pungent flavour, you can use Ezine *beyaz peynir* (sheep's cheese local to Ezine in Marmara; or use feta) or Erzincan *tulum peyniri* (goat's milk cheese local to Erzincan in Anatolia; or use fontina).

While wrapping the *börek* (savoury pastry)

I divide each piece of *yufka* (or filo/phyllo pastry) into 8 triangular sections. I place a tablespoon of the stuffing along the long edge of each piece. Then I fold the sides of the triangle inward and roll the *yufka* around the stuffing loosely so that it resembles a small log.

Heating the hazelnut oil to 180°C (350°F), the ideal temperature for frying *yufka*, I fry each *börek* until it is golden yellow. I place each *börek* on a paper towel to absorb any excess oil and then I serve them.

You can serve *börek* stuffed with vegetables and strained yoghurt if you wish.

* *soft, uncured cheese*

Purslane salad with tahini and hazelnuts

2 bunches of purslane
   (or watercress)
50 g (1.75 oz) tahini
Juice of 1 lemon
1 clove of garlic
5 g (0.17 oz/1 tsp) cumin
A pinch of red pepper
Salt
Extra-virgin olive oil
100 g (3.5 oz/very generous
   ½ cup) hazelnuts

4 SERVINGS

After soaking the purslane (or watercress) in water, I rinse it thoroughly and put it in a sieve to dry. I remove the stems because they are thick.

I beat the tahini, lemon juice, crushed garlic, cumin, red pepper and salt in a small bowl. Adding just a bit of olive oil, I bring the mixture to the consistency of a sauce. If I think the sauce is too thick, I thin it with a few drops of water.

I bake the hazelnuts at 150°C (300°F/Gas 2) for 15 minutes and then chop them after they have cooled. Alternatively, you can crush them with a pestle and mortar, but don't make them too fine.

I mix the dried purslane with the sauce in a deep bowl. Adding the hazelnuts and mixing once again, I transfer the salad to salad bowls and serve.

Char-grilled vegetable salad with basil

3 aubergines (eggplants)
5 green peppers
2 spring onions (scallions)
3 tomatoes
½ a lemon
10 ml (0.3 fl oz/2 tsp) vinegar
Salt
Freshly ground black pepper
2 cloves of garlic
Extra-virgin olive oil
1 bunch of basil

4-6 SERVINGS

In our kitchen, we char-grill all vegetables so we get that wonderful smoky flavour you can't get from baking them. Depending on what you have available, you can char-grill on a griddle, a stove or a barbecue.

I char-grill the aubergines (eggplants) first because they take a long time. Then I do the peppers, spring onions (scallions) and, finally, the tomatoes. I grill (broil) them until all sides have become soft and they can be peeled easily. I place the char-grilled pepper, spring onions (scallions) and tomatoes into a large bowl and seal it with plastic wrap. This makes the vegetables sweat and so easier to peel.

I peel the char-grilled aubergines (eggplants) and coat them with lemon juice to keep them from browning. Then I cut the peeled aubergines (eggplants), pepper, spring onions (scallions) and tomatoes as small as possible and, while still warm, I mix them with vinegar, salt, crushed garlic, freshly ground black pepper and extra-virgin olive oil. I chop the basil finely and mix it with the vegetables.

I serve this salad warm if possible. If I need to put it into the refrigerator to consume later, I let it reach room temperature again before serving. If I prepare this salad for the next day, I withhold the garlic until just before serving because the flavour of the garlic becomes too intense if it is kept in the refrigerator for that long.

Mussels steamed in *rakı*

500 g (1 lb 2 oz)
    small mussels
2 cloves of garlic
½ an onion
Olive oil
2 sprigs of parsley
2 bay leaves
50 ml (2 fl oz/¼ cup)
    rakı * (or Pernod)
50 g (1.75 oz/½ stick)
    butter, diced
Albanian pepper (or red
    pepper flakes; optional)
Salt
1 tomato

**Flavours that
complement mussels**

Butter, hot pepper,
garlic, cream,
lemon, olive oil,
onion, saffron,
fresh oregano,
tomato, white wine
and leeks

4 SERVINGS

I set aside the mussels I have cleaned and, if it is warm, I place them in the refrigerator. I dice the garlic and onion very finely and I sauté them for a few minutes in olive oil in a medium-large pan. I add the mussels, the parsley stems and bay leaves, using a wooden spoon to mix them. Then I add the *rakı* * (or Pernod) to the mixture. I cover the pan and shake it and continue cooking for 5-8 minutes until the shells have opened.

Once the mussels have released their juices, I add butter, a bit of Albanian pepper (or red pepper flakes), salt and the tomato, which I have diced finely. The Albanian pepper makes this dish hot, which I like, but you can omit it if you prefer. As the butter melts in the juice of the mussels, the sauce becomes thicker. If you prefer a more watery dish, you can add 125 ml (4.4 fl oz/½ cup) of water alongside the *rakı*.

* *an aniseed-flavoured Turkish spirit*

MUSSELS
I make sure that the mussels are alive and I do this by choosing only those that have closed shells; dead mussels have open shells. Clean the 'beards' off them with a wire scouring pad or the back of a knife. Remove all strands of 'beard' so they will not bother you when you are eating them. Don't eat mussels in May, June, July or August since that is their breeding season and the risk of poisoning is greater then.

Dusky grouper baked in milk

1 litre (34 fl oz/1 quart) milk
2 cloves of garlic
2 celery stalks
1 bunch of dill
2 bay leaves
2 fig leaves
Freshly ground black pepper
Salt
2 sprigs of fresh oregano
1 kg (2 lb 4 oz) dusky grouper
    (or grouper or halibut)
1 handful of dill

DUSKY GROUPER
Dusky grouper
generally inhabits
rocks and holes. It comes
close to shore in summer
and its skin is thick
and firm.

4 SERVINGS

I boil the peeled garlic, celery stalk, dill, bay leaves, fig leaves, freshly ground black pepper, salt and oregano in milk on a low heat for half an hour and then I strain the milk.

I fillet the fish (see the recipe for sea bass for how to do this, p. 256). I keep the head to make soup. I place the fish into a large deep baking dish, skin-side down, then I pour the strained milk over the fish and bake it for 10-15 minutes at 160°C (320°F). Once cooked, I sprinkle chopped dill on top and serve.

You can add saffron or onion, according to taste. The herbs are fresh, so I prefer to use them in light evening meals.

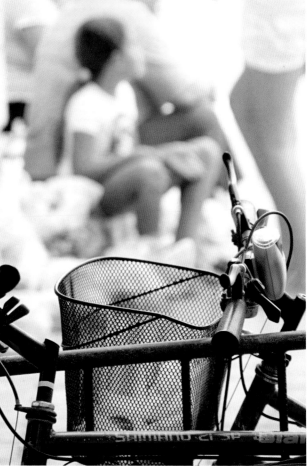

YALIKAVAK

BODRUM *holds a special place in my heart. I'm not sure why—perhaps because of all my summertime experiences in my high school days, or the fact that my aunt lives there, or the pleasure I get from island-hopping around the peninsula. I just don't know. Every time I take the winding road from Güvercinlik to the town, the fish farms and islets of varying sizes on my right bring a smile of pleasure to my face. The innumerable memories and feelings I harbour are probably why I am so passionate about this town.*

On this visit to the Bodrum Peninsula, I'm going to take you to the market in Yalıkavak, on the north-west coast. Actually, everyday nearly every bay around the Bodrum Peninsula hosts a market and Thursdays are Yalıkavak's turn. Though the market in Turgutreis is the biggest, the Yalıkavak market is more colourful. In summer, the marketplace instils an amazing feeling in visitors; it is like big-city-dwellers come here to quench their thirst for nature. In no other market have I seen so many elegant, well-groomed women in one place and I can't decide whether to look at them or busy myself with buying supplies. The stallholders speak English and this attracts tourists who, rather than buy anything, are enthralled by the kaleidoscope of local colour. The real reason for my coming here are the fabulous vegetables, fruit, cotton flannel clothes and jams.

Shaking off summer fatigue to make yet another trip to the market, I find some important changes. Amid that medley of colours, there is a serene marketplace filled with the fragrance of citrus. The fragrance of Bodrum's oranges and tangerines tickles my nose in a special way. I buy a bag of satsumas: some for juice and the rest for a salad dressing. After a busy summer, the stallholders are in a pleasant daze and their faces are relaxed. The women selling butter have shawls over their shoulders because of the cool weather. I love the energy of this season.

I load my purchases into the car. Instead of repeating my previous visit's quick lunch of köfte *(traditional Turkish meatballs), I set off south along the coast for Gümüşlük for a more relaxed, pleasant meal. The sun's rays are lower in the sky and balmier than in the height of summer and, with a light breeze, the rays soothe my soul. Alone, I have a* rakı *(Turkish aniseed-flavoured spirit) and a lovely lunch of a few* meze *(small dishes) and grilled squid, and delight in the seaside ambiance of Gümüşlük.*

Dishes capturing the flavours of Yalıkavak market
- Aubergine salad with tahini, 136
- Baked seafood with orange and dill, 138
- Brain with purslane salad, 140
- Leerfish schnitzel and crushed potatoes with herbs, 142
- Watercress soup with toast, 144
- Greens with tangerine dressing, 147
- Apple and beetroot soup, 148
- Meringue with bergamot-flavoured chocolate sauce and ice cream, 150

Aubergine salad with tahini

8 plump aubergines
   (eggplant)
1 lemon
100 g (3.5 oz) tahini
3 cloves of garlic
3 g (0.1 oz/generous tsp)
   cumin
3 g (0.1 oz/generous tsp)
   paprika
Olive oil

4 SERVINGS

I prefer char-grilling aubergines (eggplant).
I recommend using a wood oven for this recipe
because the woodsmoke permeates the aubergines
(eggplant), making this *meze* (small dish) even
more delicious. I char-grill the aubergines
(eggplant) until their skins are burned nearly
all over and their flesh is very soft, then I peel
them and put them into a bowl. I squeeze lemon
juice on them to keep them from darkening.
I love aubergines (eggplant) whole but, if you
want, you can cut them into small pieces.

I add the tahini, crushed garlic, cumin and paprika
to the still slightly warm aubergines (eggplant)
and mix. I add salt to taste. Then I gradually
drizzle olive oil into the mixture. I leave the olive
oil till last because if I put the olive oil in first,
the aubergines (eggplant) won't absorb the flavour
of the other ingredients.

Because of the intense flavour the tahini gives to
this aubergine (eggplant) salad, I prefer to serve it
on days that are not too hot. It can stand alone as a
meze (small dish) or, when served warm, it goes well
with meat and chicken.

Baked seafood with orange and dill

For the fish stock

Fish heads and bones

2 litres (68 fl oz/2 quarts)
    water

1 onion

1 leek

1 bay leaf

5 black peppercorns

200 ml (7 fl oz/scant 1 cup)
    white wine

For the casserole sauce

2 onions

Olive oil

Salt

1 bay leaf

2 cloves of garlic

1 orange

300 ml (10 fl oz/1¼ cups)
    fish stock

1 bunch of parsley stems

Freshly ground black pepper

For the casserole

4 pieces of octopus, cooked

8 mussels

4 pieces of sea bass

8 shrimp

20 g (¾ oz/1 heaped tbsp)
    butter

1 bunch of dill

4 slices of *köy ekmeği* *
    (or sour dough)

4-6 SERVINGS

For the fish stock

To make the fish stock, I boil the head and bones
of a large fish in water with an onion, a leek, a bay
leaf, the black peppercorns and white wine for half
an hour. If you have no other ingredients to make
this stock, you can use water alone, but remember
that a rich fish stock adds a distinct flavour to
the dish.

For the casserole sauce

To make the sauce, I cut the onions into long, thin
strips and sauté them in olive oil in a medium-sized
pan. I sprinkle some salt on the onions to release
their juices. Then I add the bay leaf and garlic. After
squeezing the juice from the orange, I add it to the
pan and I cook it on a medium heat until the juice
has been absorbed. I add the fish stock and parsley
stems and I boil it for 10 minutes. Finally, I stir in
some freshly ground black pepper.

Preparing the casserole

I put the cooked octopus (see the recipe for sautéed
octopus on p. 44), mussels, fillets of sea bass, shrimp
and butter into a casserole dish, cover them all
with the casserole sauce, and I bake the dish for 20
minutes at 180°C (350°F/Gas 4). I cover the casserole
with finely chopped dill and serve with toast.

** village bread, a simple flat bread prepared on a hot
plate, not baked*

Brain with purslane salad

1 lamb's brain
A few drops of vinegar
5 litres (5 quarts) cold water
Salt
2 bay leaves
Black peppercorns
A few drops of vinegar
Salt
2 lemons
200 ml (7 fl oz/scant 1 cup)
    extra-virgin olive oil
Freshly ground black pepper
2 bunches of purslane
    (or watercress)
3 drops of wine vinegar

4 SERVINGS

I soak a lamb's brain in 3 litres (101 fl oz/3 quarts) of water mixed with vinegar overnight in the refrigerator. I recommend soaking offal in vinegar to extract the blood. I remove the brain's outer membrane before cooking because it is easier than doing it after. I put the remaining 2 litres (68 fl oz/ 2 quarts) of water, bay leaves, black peppercorns, a few drops of vinegar and salt into a pan and boil the mixture. I put the brain into the boiling water for 8-10 minutes. As soon as I take the brain out of the water, I plunge it into ice water. Once it has cooled, I put it on a cutting board and cut it into slices the width of a finger. I put the brain slices on a plate and cover them with the juice of a lemon and 100 ml (3.5 fl oz/scant ½ cup) of olive oil. Finally, I add freshly ground black pepper.

After washing and drying the purslane (or watercress), I mix it with the remaining 100 ml (3.5 fl oz/scant ½ cup) of olive oil, the juice of a lemon and the wine vinegar. I serve the slices of brain with purslane salad on the side.

Brain has the highest proportion of cholesterol of all offal.

To prepare a relatively light appetizer, I wait for the months of spring, when the lambs are at their most tender. I prefer lamb brain as a salad rather than breaded and fried.

Leerfish schnitzel and crushed potatoes with herbs

For the crushed potatoes

½ kg (1 lb 2 oz) fresh
    potatoes, small
Water
Salt
2 lemons
Olive oil
1 bunch of parsley
1 bunch of dill

For the leerfish schnitzel

1.2 kg (1 lb 11 oz) leerfish
    (or cod or yellowtail)
Salt
Freshly ground black pepper
100 g (3.5 oz/scant 1 cup)
    flour
3 eggs
100 g (3.5 oz) breadcrumbs
Hazelnut oil for frying

4 SERVINGS

For the crushed potatoes

I wash the fresh potatoes with plenty of water. Without peeling them, I put them in a pan with 2 litres (68 fl oz/2 quarts) of water and some salt, and boil them until they are soft inside. The cooking period should be about 25 minutes, but it will depend on the type of potato. I stab the potatoes with a small wooden skewer to check on their progress. While the potatoes are still warm, I add a mixture of lemon juice, olive oil and plenty of dill and parsley and mash them all together.

For the schnitzel

I make sure that the leerfish (or cod or yellowtail) I buy for our kitchen are over 10 kg (22 lb) because that size gives enough white meat. If you don't want to buy such a large fish, you can have the amount you desire cut from one. From leerfish fillets, I get 4 logs and I separate them into 300 g (10.5 oz) slices. I pound them into thinner rounds with a meat tenderizing hammer until they are about 2 mm (1/16 in) thick and a lot wider in diameter. It is useful to pound the fish between 2 pieces of plastic wrap. After seasoning the fish slices with salt and freshly ground black pepper, I dust them with flour and then I dip them into the beaten eggs. Finally, I coat them with breadcrumbs. I fill a large frying pan half full with hazelnut oil and bring it to a high temperature. Then I fry each side of the pounded fish slices for approximately 2 minutes until they are quite brown.

I serve leerfish schnitzel with potato puree with herbs on the side.

Meats that make good schnitzel
Rump of beef,
chicken breast
and beef tongue

Watercress soup with toast

4 large potatoes
3 leeks
30 g (1 oz/2 tbsp) butter
2 litres (68 fl oz/2 quarts)
    water
Salt
Freshly ground black pepper
1 bunch of watercress
4 slices of bread

4 SERVINGS

After peeling the potatoes, I submerge them whole in water to prevent them blackening.

I clean the leeks by first letting them soak in plenty of water for half an hour, then I wash them, making sure to remove any soil trapped between the leaves. After cleaning the leeks, I slice them into thin rings, then I sauté them in butter in a medium-sized pan on a medium heat. Meanwhile, I dice the potatoes.

I boil water and add it to the leeks. Then I put the potatoes in with the leeks, add salt and pepper and boil the whole on a low heat until the potatoes are cooked: about 35-40 minutes. Then I puree the contents of the pan with a hand blender. I place the washed watercress into the pan and blend again until it is an emerald-green soup. I serve straight away in bowls with toast. I love to have this soup with plenty of freshly ground black pepper.

This soup uses potatoes as a thickener instead of flour, so you can also serve it cold. This recipe is for a light summer soup, but if want to make a thick winter soup, just add some cream. I like using rocket instead of watercress in this recipe. If you wish, sorrel, mixed herbs or tender spinach can be used instead of watercress.

Greens with tangerine dressing

1 bunch of watercress
1 bunch of rocket
1 bunch of sorrel
4 leaves of lettuce
1 bunch of purslane
3 sprigs of fresh mint
3 sprigs of parsley

For the tangerine dressing
4 tangerines
1 lemon
Salt
Freshly ground black pepper
1 spring onion (scallion)
Early harvest olive oil
50 g (1.75 oz) curds for a
    topping (or cottage
    cheese; if desired)

4 SERVINGS

For the tangerine dressing

If you buy tangerines in the fall, their insides will
have a richer orange colour and a more pungent
fragrance than at other times. I squeeze the
tangerines and lemon to get their juice. To the
juice, I add salt, freshly ground black pepper, spring
onion (scallion) cut into long thin strands and olive
oil and I mix them. I let the mixture sit for
10-15 minutes so that the ingredients can mingle.

I wash and sort the greens. I like using these greens
together because the bitterness of watercress and
rocket, the tartness of purslane and sorrel, the
neutrality of lettuce, and the flavour of mint and
parsley balance each other. I especially choose mint
for salads because it adds a fresh zest.

Wet salad leaves cannot absorb the dressing, so
I dry the washed greens thoroughly with either
a paper towel or a salad dryer. Also, the dressing
should be thoroughly combined with the salad
because a dressing that is simply drizzled over the
salad does not distribute itself evenly. I keep the
mixed greens in one container and the dressing in
another and combine the two just before serving,
then I add the curds (or cottage cheese).

Apple and beetroot soup

1 onion
30 g (1 oz/2 tbsp) butter
30 ml (1 fl oz/2 tbsp) olive oil
5 large beetroot (beets)
1 litre (34 fl oz/1 quart)
    apple juice
1 litre (34 fl oz/1 quart) water
Salt
Freshly ground black pepper
20 ml (¾ fl oz/1 generous
    tbsp) fresh cream
1 spring onion (scallion)

8 SERVINGS

I dice the onion finely. I put the olive oil into a medium-sized pan and melt in the butter on a moderate flame, then I sauté the onions. After skinning and dicing the beetroot (beets), I add them to the onions and continue sautéing.

I add the apple juice, salt and freshly ground black pepper and cook the mixture on a low heat for an hour, until the beetroot (beets) has become very soft. I puree the mixture with a hand blender and I add a spoonful of fresh cream on top. I serve with pieces of spring onion (scallion) that I have cut lengthwise.

I like serving this light soup cold in shot glasses, too. I prefer using apple juice, but you may add a few slices of apple and blend them with the other ingredients instead.

Flavourings that complement beetroot

Apple, butter, cheese, garlic, honey, lemon, mustard, vinegar and walnuts

Meringue with bergamot-flavoured chocolate sauce and ice cream

4 SERVINGS

For the topping

1 small bergamot (or try aromatic tangerine)

500 ml (18 fl oz/2¼ cups) cream

300 g (10.5 oz) bitter chocolate

500 g (1 lb 2 oz) chocolate ice cream

Fresh mint leaves, to garnish

For the meringue

8 egg whites

450 g (1 lb/2¼ cups) granulated sugar

2 drops of vinegar

For the bergamot-flavoured chocolate sauce

I grate the skin of a bergamot (or aromatic tangerine) and put half of the gratings with cream into a small pan. I love the pungent aroma of bergamot in this dessert. If I wanted a slightly less powerful aroma, I would use a quarter of the grated skin. I boil the gratings and cream on low heat for 15-20 minutes, stirring from time to time to ensure that the bergamot aroma permeates the cream. Then I add the chocolate, which I have broken into small pieces, to the boiling cream and stir with a wooden spoon until it has melted.

I leave the sauce at room temperature. This sauce can keep at room temperature for 1-2 days; any longer and it will need refrigeration. If the sauce is refrigerated, it will need re-warming before it is used.

For the meringue

I beat the egg whites and I gradually add granulated sugar, then the vinegar. The whites are ready once they gain the consistency of firm snow.

I set the oven at 120°C (250°F) and I evenly space individual spoonfuls of the meringue mix onto a baking tray covered in baking paper. I bake for 40-45 minutes, until the meringue is chewy on the inside and crispy on the outside.

Preparing the plate

I break up the meringue into pieces and put them into glasses or a large bowl. I put chocolate ice cream on them and I drizzle the bergamot-flavoured chocolate sauce over the top. Finally, I garnish the dish with fresh mint leaves.

MUĞLA

HAVRAN

ALAÇATI
URLA

TİRE

MİLAS

MUĞLA

YALIKAVAK

ULA

MARMARİS

DATÇA

BOZBURUN

THURSDAY *is market day in Muğla. The city is surrounded by dozens of villages and towns and, with practice, you can begin to distinguish the stallholders' origins from their faces, the easiest being those of people from Aydın, Koçarlı, Ula, Çineliler and Kızılağaçlılar.*

Markets drawing sellers from such a wide and varied region offer an equally wide range of products. Muğla market is no exception, with a plentiful range of produce in its many sections, throwing the products of the plains alongside those of the hills. In my experience as an inveterate market-goer, prices are lower here than at any other market.

There are two types of market stallholders: those who sell their own produce and those who sell the produce of others. The producer-sellers have an immediate and apparent bond with their produce and they dominate this market. It is difficult to bargain with them, and the labour they have put into their produce is reflected in the tender care they give to its presentation on their stalls.

Muğla's haphazard development, apparent from a distance, disturbs me. But once I enter this crowded market and wander around the stalls, my unease falls away. The structure of the houses, the narrow streets, the tinsmiths, second-hand dealers and nut sellers arrayed along the streets lift my spirits.

Taking advantage of my father accompanying me, I go to a köfteci (meatball restaurant) in the Sanayi neighbourhood, a place I would never have visited by myself, and I experience something completely unexpected there. Near a mosque and hidden behind vines, the köfteci (meatball restaurant) had only three tables. The owners— a father and son—make and grill (broil) köfte (traditional Turkish meatball) the size of a 1 lira coin, mix them with onion and tomatoes seasoned with sumac, and cook the whole into a juicy dish. They serve it with ox-milk yoghurt and warm bread baked in a wood-fired oven. After this feast, we hit the road again.

The roads to Muğla market are at least as much fun as the market itself. My favourite road is the one we used to take from Sakar Mountain to Gökova. Ahead you see Gökova Gulf, in the distance to the left Köyceğiz Lake, and below that is a huge plain. The plain is of breathless beauty and the markets are an excuse to go this way again.

Dishes capturing the flavours of Muğla market
- Raw sea bass with fresh tomatoes and extra-virgin olive oil, 156
- White grouper on sautéed artichokes, 158
- Lamb shanks with chickpeas, 160
- Candied quince with *tulum peyniri*, 162
- Flavoured butters: dried tomatoes and walnuts, dill and lemon, honey and lavender, 164
- Hot-smoked lamb loins with mustard sauce and caramelized onion, 166
- Chocolate truffles with chestnuts, 168
- Crispy chicken with spicy honey sauce, 170
- Grilled fruit with *kaymak* and walnuts, 172

Raw sea bass with fresh tomatoes and extra-virgin olive oil

1 kg (2 lb 4 oz) sea bass
Sea salt
Freshly ground black pepper
2 large tomatoes
Spring onion (scallion)
Extra-virgin olive oil

4 SERVINGS

Eating raw fish may seem alien to Turkish culture, but in fact Turks are used to eating salted fish as a *meze* (small dish). We like eating salted bonito and mackerel. I have a predilection for eating raw fish that I have 'cooked' by soaking in lemon or salt or simply by seasoning with a bit of salt and a little olive oil. In the heat of summer, when I want something light to eat, I prefer raw fish to cooked fish. If the idea of raw fish is unfamiliar to you, before throwing your fish on a grill, cut off a piece, mix it with lemon, salt and olive oil and eat it. I believe you will like it.

Make sure that the sea bass you use for this recipe is large and fatty. Fillet it by running a knife next to the bone and parallel to the work surface, working one side of the bone, turning the fish over and then working the other. I cut both fillets into very thin slices. To ensure that the slices are of an adequate width, I hold the knife at 120 degrees rather than at right angles to the cutting board.

I place the fish slices on a plate I have sprinkled with salt and freshly ground black pepper. I sprinkle the top of the fish with salt, too. I grate tomato and cover the fish with it. I serve the fish with a lot of extra-virgin olive oil, freshly ground pepper, and spring onions (scallions) cut diagonally.

You can prepare the same dish with cod, Leerfish, white grouper or dusky grouper. You should make this dish immediately before serving since it is inadvisable to keep it for any period, in or out of the refrigerator.

PREPARING RAW FISH

Salt and lemon 'cook' raw fish. The salt helps release the juice of the fish while the acid in the lemon 'cooks' the fish meat. In this recipe, the citric acid's function is performed by tomatoes. The most important aspect of preparing raw fish is the choice of fish. The eyes of the fish should be like glass and its gills should be blood-red. Though it is important that all fish be fresh, fish for eating raw must have been caught that day. Don't try using frozen fish because the enzymes formed while the fish is frozen and defrosted pose a risk when fish is eaten raw, even if it does not when cooked.

White grouper on sautéed artichokes

4 artichokes
50 ml (2 fl oz/scant ¼ cup)
    olive oil
1 lemon
Water
Salt
Freshly ground black pepper
4 g (0.14 oz/1 tsp) sugar
½ a bunch of dill
1 kg (2 lb 4 oz) white grouper
    (or grouper or halibut)
Olive oil
Salt
Freshly ground black pepper

4 SERVINGS

It is best to buy artichokes when they are in season (see right), as canned artichokes are not as good as fresh ones. I place the cleaned artichokes in a wide pan with the olive oil, add the juice of a freshly squeezed lemon and enough water to come halfway up the artichokes. I add salt and freshly ground black pepper, cover the pan and cook the artichokes on a medium heat. Once the artichokes are soft, I take the lid off and increase the heat slightly and begin caramelizing the artichokes by adding a small amount of sugar. I sprinkle finely chopped dill on the browned artichokes and turn them over.

I have my fishmonger fillet the grouper (or halibut). I cut 200 g (7 oz) portions of the fillet and rub salt and pepper into them. I cook the fish in olive oil that I added to a very hot non-stick pan. I serve the dish when both sides are golden, with a side dish of caramelized artichokes.

You can also put grated Bergama *tulum peyniri** (or emmenthal) or a fatty and hard *kaşar*** (or gruyère) over the top of the artichokes. If you do, you can use the artichokes as a garnish with chicken or meat.

* *unpasteurized, soft-ripened goat's/sheep's milk cheese local to Bergama in İzmir province in Turkey*
** *unpasteurized, medium-hard sheep's/cow's milk cheese*

ARTICHOKES
Artichokes are perennial thistles with beautiful purple flowers.
The part we eat is taken from the artichoke bud, the 'choke'. Artichoke harvesting begins in May and extends to the end of June. Once trimmed and ready to use, submerge the chokes in water containing lemon juice to prevent them from browning.

Lamb shanks with chickpeas

300 g (10.5 oz) chickpeas
1 litre (34 fl oz/1 quart)
   cold water
2 onions
2 bay leaves
1 litre (34 fl oz/1 quart)
   boiling water
20 g (¾ oz/1 heaped tbsp)
   butter
1 sprig of rosemary
Salt
Freshly ground black pepper
4 lamb shanks

4 SERVINGS

I soak the chickpeas in water overnight, then drain them and add fresh water equivalent to about 3 times the weight of the chickpeas (in this case, about 1 litre (34 fl oz/1 quart) and boil them for 20 minutes. I add a bay leaf and a peeled, whole onion. I don't add salt because it toughens legumes and lengthens cooking time. I cut the remaining onion into thin slices, put them into another pan and sauté them in butter. I add rosemary, the remaining bay leaf, salt and freshly ground black pepper and stir. I put the lamb and 1 litre (34 fl oz/ 1 quart) of boiling water into this pan and leave it to simmer. After 30 minutes, I strain the half-cooked chickpeas and put them into the pan with the lamb and cook the entire mixture for another hour. I prefer to serve lamb shank on the bone because the marrow and the bone enhance the flavour of the broth.

In my restaurant, I serve this ideal winter dish with rice cooked with *şehriye* (or vermicelli), a common Turkish combination. If you prefer, you can simply serve it with toast.

Candied quince with *tulum peyniri*

4 quinces
1 kg (2 lb 4 oz/5 cups)
   granulated sugar
½ a lemon
2 cloves
200 g (7 oz) *tulum peyniri* *
   (or emmenthal)
½ a loaf of *köy ekmeği* **
   (or baguette/French
   bread)
Freshly ground black pepper

4 SERVINGS

I prefer to grate the peeled quince before I cook it but, if I want the candy to keep for months, I dice the quince so that it keeps longer. I mix the grated quince and sugar together and let it sit for 2-3 hours. Once the juice has been released, I put the quince-sugar mix into a large pan, add lemon and cloves and boil it. From time to time I skim off the foam that forms while the mixture is boiling. The candied quince is ready when it is thicker than jam, which takes 45-60 minutes.

I serve candied quince with thinly sliced, toasted *köy ekmeği* ** and *tulum peyniri* *.

When preparing a cheese plate, I include walnuts, prunes and raisins. Depending on the season, fresh figs and fragrant strawberries also go well with a cheese plate.

* *unpasteurized, soft-ripened goat's/sheep's milk cheese*
** *village bread, a simple flat bread prepared on a hot
   plate, not baked*

Flavoured butters: dried tomatoes and walnuts, dill and lemon, honey and lavender

250 g (9 oz/generous 1 cup)
    butter
50 g (1.75 oz/scant ½ cup)
    walnuts
Fresh oregano
4 dried tomatoes
Salt

250 g (9 oz/generous 1 cup)
    butter
2 lemon rinds
½ a bunch of dill
Salt

250 g (9 oz/generous 1 cup)
    butter
50 g (1.75 oz/generous
    2 tbsp) honey
3 sprigs of lavender

I let the butter stand for a while at room temperature to make it easier to mix with the other ingredients. It is not very practical to try to blend them with butter that is too cold or that has melted too much.

You can prepare butter with garlic, onion, parsley, curry, saffron, cumin, fresh coriander (cilantro), crushed coriander seeds, orange rind, capers and many other aromatic ingredients.

Butter flavoured with dried tomato and walnut

I mix the walnuts, fresh oregano and dried tomatoes in a food processor and gradually add the butter. If I want salty butter, I add a pinch of salt during the mixing. I use this butter at breakfast and for sandwiches.

Butter flavoured with dill and grated lemon rind

I grate the lemon rind finely and chop the dill finely. Then I mix the ingredients.

I use this seasoned butter for canapés of smoked fish and in sandwiches. I put it on leerfish (or cod or yellowtail) schnitzel (see p. 142) and serve. Unsalted butter is better with smoked fish, because there is enough salt in the fish.

Butter flavoured with honey and lavender

I separate the lavender flowers from their stems and I fold them in with the honey and butter at room temperature.

Hot-smoked lamb loins with mustard sauce and caramelized onion

8 lamb loins
10 g (¼ oz/2 tsp) salt
10 g (¼ oz/2 tsp) granulated
  sugar
4 onions
Olive oil
Salt
20 g (¾ oz/1 heaped tbsp)
  granulated sugar
50 g (1.75 oz/2 tbsp)
  Dijon mustard
50 g (1.75 oz/2 generous
  tbsp) honey

4 SERVINGS

The best way to hot-smoke food is in a smoking box, but if you don't have one, you can do it using a covered grill or a pan. The wood chips are all important because chips from different trees produce different aromas to flavour the food. Oak is the best. I also like incense (storax) wood. There are only a few of these trees in the world and they grow on the Datça Peninsula, so I think we have a unique opportunity to use this wood. However, if you would like a slightly sweet taste to your smoked meat, use wood from fruit trees. I don't recommend pine wood because its aroma is not pleasant and it burns quickly.

The trick is to ensure that the hot smoke reaches the food I am slowly cooking while the smoke's aroma complements, but does not smother, the food's own flavour. To release the juices of the meat, I let it sit in salt and sugar beforehand, and then the smoke can permeate the meat more easily.

I have the sinew of the loins removed and dust the fillet with salt and sugar in a container that I seal with plastic wrap and place in the refrigerator for 12 hours. When I'm ready to smoke it, I place 2 handfuls of wood shavings in a large, wide pan

and position a small grill above them, place the meat on the grill and cover it. I put the closed pan on the stove and cook the meat for 15 minutes on a low heat. I serve when the meat is medium-rare.

You can also prepare this dish in a covered barbecue with a small amount of charcoal.

To caramelize the onions, I cut them into long, thin slices and sauté them in a non-stick pan with a little olive oil for 15-20 minutes until brown. I add salt and sugar and continually stir as they cook.

I mix honey and mustard in a bowl and then pour the mixture over the loins. You can also use mustard without honey. I serve the lamb loins with caramelized onion on the side.

I like to use the same recipe with turkey, chicken, fish, or beef instead of lamb.

Chocolate truffles with chestnuts

250 g (9 oz) chestnuts
1 litre (34 fl oz/1 quart)
    cold water
50 g (1.75 oz/scant
    ½ cup) icing sugar
    (confectioners' sugar)
100 ml (3.5 fl oz/scant
    ½ cup) cream
200 g (7 oz) bitter chocolate
    (70% cocoa)
5 g (0.17 oz/1 tsp) butter
100 g (3.5 oz/very generous
    ½ cup) cocoa

4 SERVINGS

I wash the chestnuts. Then I make a small incision on the flat side of each chestnut shell. I place the chestnuts in a pan with 1 litre (34 fl oz/1 quart) of cold water and bring it to the boil and keep it boiling for 35-40 minutes. Once the chestnuts have become completely soft, I drain the water and remove the shells. I place the chestnuts with the icing sugar (confectioners' sugar) in a food processor and puree them.

I boil the cream and mix in small pieces of chocolate with a wooden spoon. To get the cream to firm-up more easily, I add butter and the chestnut puree. I mix all of them and put the mixture into the refrigerator, where I let it sit for about 40 minutes.

I scoop out the firm mixture with a soup spoon, rolling each spoonful in the palm of my hand as I go. Once the mixture is used up, I cover the balls with cocoa and put them into the refrigerator.

I serve these truffles with coffee.

Crispy chicken with spicy honey sauce

The meat of 4 chicken thighs
150 ml (5.5 fl oz/generous
 ½ cup) *ayran* (or drinking
 yoghurt)
50 ml (2 fl oz/¼ cup) milk
1-3 drops of Tabasco sauce
Salt
Wheat flour
Hazelnut oil for frying
50 g (1.75 oz/generous
 2 tbsp) honey
2-3 drops of Tabasco sauce
3 g (0.1 oz/scant tsp)
 sesame seeds

4 SERVINGS

I prefer thigh and buttock meat for this recipe,
but you can also use breast or wing meat.

I mix the *ayran* (or drinking yoghurt), milk,
1-3 drops of Tabasco sauce and a pinch of salt in a
wide bowl and marinate the chicken pieces in this
mixture overnight. I cover the marinated chicken
with flour and fry it in hazelnut oil at 190°C (375°F).

I mix the honey, 2-3 drops of Tabasco sauce and
sesame seeds and serve it with the chicken as a dip.
I also like eating crispy chicken with mustard.

Children love this dish, though I may leave out the
Tabasco sauce if it makes it too hot for them.

Grilled fruit with *kaymak* and walnuts

100 g (3.5 oz/scant 1 cup)
 walnuts
250 g (9 oz) fresh *kaymak*
 (or clotted cream; see
 box)
1 peach
2 apricots
2 fresh figs
Olive oil
100 g (3.5 oz/scant
 ⅓ cup) honey

4 SERVINGS

KAYMAK

I recommend *kaymak* made from water buffalo milk for its strong flavour. However, though it takes 2 days to make, it only keeps for a further 2. The *kaymak* sold in supermarkets that stays fresh for 10 days is not made with buffalo milk, but from the cream of cows' milk. Getting milk from water buffalo is difficult: the animal only produces milk reliably if it is kept where it was born and receives the love and attention of its owner. These stringent requirements are making water buffalo husbandry a rarity and make their *kaymak* even more expensive than that of industrially farmed cows. If I need large quantities of *kaymak*, I still buy it in small cartons because, once a carton is opened, the milk separates and the *kaymak* loses its freshness more rapidly.

I chop the walnuts finely and gradually add them to the *kaymak* (or clotted cream). I put the mixture into the refrigerator.

I cut the fruit in half down the middle and remove the seeds from the peach and apricots. I cover the fruit sparingly with olive oil and pour a bit of honey over them. Then I place them on a red-hot grill and cook each side for 2 minutes. I serve them with the *kaymak*.

ULA

HAVRAN

ALAÇATI

URLA

TİRE

MİLAS

MUĞLA

YALIKAVAK

ULA

MARMARİS

DATÇA

BOZBURUN

ULA IS a small town between Muğla and Gökova, graced each Friday by an equally small market where talkative senior citizens sell the freshest produce of the week on narrow stalls. It is a real village market, with hardly any produce coming from outside.

I and two members of our kitchen crew set off early. We find an elderly woman sitting on a stool at her stall selling her own butter, süzme (thickened) yoghurt and curd. We are surrounded by an abundance of dried herbs: sage, lavender, oregano flowers and a long, thin herb with sprigs, called sılcan, a plant rather like purslane that is eaten sautéed. It grows in the woods under amber trees and in water and it is found from the mid-April to November. I buy a few bunches to sauté. Later, I catch sight of huge, long okra, just right for pickling and I throw 1 kilo (2 lb 4 oz) into my bag. A woman is selling heaps of mountain lilac in large yoghurt containers. I buy the lot and fill the car with the smell of sweet lilac for the return. I see wheat, sweetcorn (corn), barley and sesame seeds on a stall and I buy some wheat.

The aroma of baking bread fills our nostrils and leads us out of the market to the front of a small wood-fired bakery. Powerless to resist, we buy bread and tear off chunks to eat. We happen upon a stall of cheeses and I buy tulum peyniri *made from a mixture of goat and sheep milk and sandwich it between the hot bread in a futile attempt to satiate ourselves.*

Hunting is an autumn activity here, when it is possible to bag quail and partridge. Ula villagers also make the most of the numerous pine mushrooms that appear after autumn rains. Grilled or sautéed pine mushrooms are delicious.

The variety of fruit trees cultivated in Ula makes it an ideal place for beekeeping, and if you follow the signs for Karabörtlen on the way to Ula, you will see the exquisite fruit gardens where freestone peaches are grown for market.

Ula's elevation ensures a comfortable climate. The area is forested in red pine. If you venture along the road to Ula at sunrise during a full moon, you will have the privilege of seeing the moon setting on your left as the sun rises on your right. Ula's other wonder is its dishes.

Dishes capturing the flavours of Ula market

- Courgette gratin with rich herb seasoning, 178
- Wheat tabbouleh, 180
- Fillet with red wine sauce seasoned with savory, 182
- Quail with rosemary and mushrooms, 184
- Free-range chicken and *köy eriştesi* soup with *süzme* yoghurt, 186
- Eggy toast with peach and apricot sauté, 190
- *Hellim peyniri* shish kebab with tomatoes and red onions, 192
- Baked red pepper stuffed with *tulum peyniri* and pine nuts, 194
- Courgette fritters with cucumber and *süzme* yoghurt sauce, 196

Courgette gratin with rich herb seasoning

3 litres (101 fl oz/3 quarts)
    water
Salt
16 courgettes (zucchini),
    round, yellow and
    green ones
75 g (2.75 oz/½ cup) flour
100 g (3.5 oz/1 stick) butter
1 litre (34 fl oz/1 quart) milk
Salt
Freshly ground black pepper
1 bunch of dill
1 bunch of spring onions
    (scallions)
150 g (5.5 oz) white cheese
    (or feta)
100 g (3.5 oz) fresh *kaşar
    peyniri* * (or gruyère)

8 SERVINGS

You can find round courgettes (zucchini) in the
market from the beginning of June until the end of
August. Because of its size, it is an ideal vegetable
to stuff. I put 3 litres (101 fl oz/3 quarts) of water
and a handful of salt into a large pan and boil the
hollowed out courgettes (zucchini) for 3-5 minutes
on a high heat. (If you are in a hurry, you can save
time by bringing the water to boil before adding
the salt.) Don't let the courgettes (zucchini) boil for
longer or they will soften too much and fall apart.

I brown the flour in butter over a low heat in a
separate saucepan. I stir in the milk gradually so as
to prevent lumps forming and, once I have a sauce
consistency, I add salt, black pepper, finely chopped
dill and spring onions (scallions). I mash the white
cheese (or feta) with a fork and gradually add it to
the sauce. Then I fill the courgettes (zucchini) with
this mixture, grate the *kaşar peyniri* * (or gruyère)
over them, and I bake them for 10-15 minutes at
180°C (350°F/Gas 4). You can serve this dish as an
entrée with salad or as a side dish with chicken.

* *unpasteurized, medium-hard sheep's/cow's milk cheese*

Wheat tabbouleh

100 g (3.5 oz) wheat
2 litres (68 fl oz/2 quarts)
    water
Salt
1 lemon
3 large tomatoes
2 small cucumbers
½ bunch of parsley
2 sprigs of fresh mint
2 spring onions (scallions)
100 ml (3.5 fl oz/scant ½
    cup) pomegranate syrup
1 clove of garlic
100 ml (3.5 fl oz/scant
    ½ cup) olive oil
Salt

4 SERVINGS

I soak the wheat in three times its weight of water for 12 hours. Then I drain it, turn it out into a saucepan containing 2 litres (68 fl oz/2 quarts) of fresh water and I boil it for about 1 hour at medium heat. Once the wheat has become *al dente*, I drain it and rinse it in cold water to remove the excess starch. I add salt and lemon juice, mix it and set it aside.

I dice the unpeeled tomatoes and cucumbers. I chop the parsley, mint and spring onions (scallions) finely and mix them into the wheat. Then I blend in the pomegranate syrup, crushed garlic and olive oil and serve.

Tabbouleh is a filling and tasty summer salad, but it also makes a nice winter salad with the addition of pomegranate instead of tomato. You can vary the herbs according to taste, using, for example, purslane, watercress or garden cress or basil.

You can also make this salad using couscous, course bulgur wheat or *orzo* (or vermicelli), or turn it into a delicious black-eyed pea salad.

Fillet with red wine sauce seasoned with savory

For the sauce
2 bottles of Öküzgözü
   grape wine (soft,
   fruity red)
30 g (1 oz/2 tbsp) honey
1 onion
3 sprigs of savory

For the fillet
700 g (1 lb 8 oz) fillet
Sea salt
Freshly ground black pepper
50 g (1.75 oz/½ stick) butter
2 sprigs of rosemary

4 SERVINGS

I reduce the wine to remove the alcohol and water and leave a thick, tasty base for the sauce. I like using honey and onion to balance the acidity of the wine. It is commonly believed that poor-quality wine can be used for sauces, but I do not agree. Wine sauce is only as tasty as the wine itself. So, even if you use a cheaper wine than normal to make sauce, you should be sure to use something better than ordinary.

I put the wine, honey and a whole unpeeled onion into a medium-sized pan and I heat the mixture for about 45 minutes on low heat. When the wine has reduced by half, I add the savory. If I were to add it at the beginning, it would make the sauce bitter. Once the wine is reduced to about a quarter of its volume, I pour the sauce on a small plate or into a sauce dish and let it cool.

The savory that grows at higher elevations, known locally as *dağ kekiği* * (or oregano), has small, pointed leaves. I like using it because it adds sharpness to a honey and wine mixture.

For the fillet

Make sure that the whole fillet that you buy is close to 2 kilos (4 lb 8 oz). The smaller the fillet, the smaller its diameter and the less juicy it will be. If possible, buy a 700 g (1 lb 8 oz) section from the middle of a whole fillet. If your butcher doesn't like this, you can buy a whole one and use the middle part of it for this recipe and the ends for sandwiches or salad. Make sure that the meat has been cleaned well before you use it.

I rub salt all over the fillet and cover it with freshly ground black pepper. I brown the meat thoroughly in a very hot frying pan for 10-12 minutes, so that the meat retains its juices. After searing the entire meat, leaving no raw parts at all, I add butter and baste the meat in it. Then I add rosemary and place the meat into a 200-220°C (400-425°F/Gas 6-7) oven and roast it for 15-20 minutes, depending on the size of the meat. If you can, use an ovenproof frying pan; if you don't have one, you will need to turn the meat out into an oven dish. When done, I cut the fillet into slices of my desired thickness and serve it in the wine sauce.

* *mountain oregano*

Quail with rosemary and mushrooms

8 quail
Salt
Freshly ground black pepper
3 sprigs of rosemary
100 ml (3.5 fl oz/scant
   ½ cup) olive oil
300 g (10.5 oz) chanterelle
   mushrooms (you can also
   use pine, morel or oyster
   mushrooms)
50 g (1.75 oz/½ stick) butter
1 onion
2 cloves of garlic
3 sprigs of parsley

4 SERVINGS

For the quail

The quail season begins at the end of August. While quail can be found at some poultry-sellers year round; the migration season begins in early autumn.

The smallest of all game birds, it is important not to let quail become dry when cooking it. It is fun to eat them with your fingers at home, but at times when this is not so acceptable, it is better to serve the quail boneless.

After washing the quail, I cut them in half. Holding the knife parallel to the cutting board, I cut out the ribcage and remove the meat. I leave the bones in the thighs. I marinate quail in salt, freshly ground black pepper, 2 sprigs of rosemary and olive oil.

For the mushrooms

If you cannot find chanterelle mushrooms, which appear after autumn rains, you can use any edible wild mushroom. I never wash mushrooms. This may seem odd to many, but mushrooms absorb water like sponges. However, you can brush, wipe or even peel them or, if you really prefer to wash them, just rinse them very quickly. Like oyster and shiitake mushrooms, the stems of chanterelle mushrooms are not eaten and they should be removed before cooking.

I cut the mushrooms lengthwise and dice the onions. I crush the garlic and chop the rosemary finely. Then I sauté the mushrooms in olive oil in a very hot frying pan. Once the mushrooms have begun to change colour, I add onion and garlic and stir rapidly. I add salt at the very end because salt draws the juices out of the mushrooms and they would tend to boil if the salt were added earlier. After seasoning with salt and freshly ground black pepper, I set the mixture aside.

Serving

I heat a frying pan and place the quail, skin-side down, in it. Once the skin has become well-browned, I turn the quail over and turn down the heat. I add butter and continue cooking until the meat is cooked thoroughly inside and out. I serve the quail with the sautéed mushrooms and garnish it with a sprinkling of chopped parsley.

Free-range chicken and *köy erişlesi* soup with *süzme* yoghurt

1 plump free-range
  chicken (heavier than
  1 kg/2 lb 4 oz)
1 onion
1 bay leaf
1 carrot
5 black peppercorns
1 sprig of rosemary
3 litres (101 fl oz/3 quarts)
  water
Salt
200 g (7 oz) *köy erişlesi* *
  (or noodles)
100 g (3.5 oz/1 stick) butter
3 g (0.1 oz/generous tsp)
  ground red pepper
2 cloves of garlic
250 g (9 oz) *süzme* yoghurt **
  (or cream cheese)

4 SERVINGS

Free-range chickens are sometimes sold in markets but, from a hygiene point of view, buying them from the butcher's is more reliable. When buying a free-range chicken, I make sure that its neck is dark yellow because this indicates that the chicken is fatty. The fattier the chicken, the more delicious is the stock made from it. Intensively-farmed chickens are overfed 6 weeks before slaughter and, though they may look plump, they are actually dry and flavourless. So, whenever possible, I choose a free-range chicken. Free-range chickens are more muscular than the intensively-farmed ones and so they need a longer cooking time, but it is worth it.

For the chicken stock

I wash the chicken thoroughly and then I hold it over a stove to singe off any remaining feathers. I put the chicken, a peeled onion, the bay leaf, carrot, black peppercorns, rosemary, water and salt into a large saucepan and boil the whole on a low heat for about 1.5-2 hours. Then, I strain the stock into another saucepan and bone the chicken. I also remove the skin and the cartilage.

For the *köy erişlesi*

I bring the chicken stock to a boil once again and, when it has started bubbling, I add the *köy erişlesi* * (or noodles) and I boil it until the noodles are soft, for about 10 minutes. I don't strain them because this is a runny dish. I prefer large *köy erişlesi* so they have a presence in this dish.

>>

Free-range chicken and *köy erişTesi* soup with *süzme* yoghurt (continued)

For the topping

I melt butter in a small frying pan until it begins to bubble and then I add the ground red pepper.

I crush the garlic and mix it into the *süzme* yoghurt ** (or cream cheese) and I ladle in some of the chicken stock. The hot stock warms up the yoghurt. I get the temperature of the yoghurt to approximate that of the dish so that it does not cool it.

Preparing the plate

I ladle the noodles into a large bowl and place the chicken pieces and the *süzme* yoghurt on top of them. I drizzle butter seasoned with ground red pepper over the top.

* *home-made noodles*
** *strained, thickened yoghurt that has been left in a cloth overnight to thicken*

Eggy toast with peach and apricot sauté

200 ml (7 fl oz/scant 1 cup)
  milk
50 g (1.75 oz/¼ cup)
  granulated sugar
3 eggs
Cinnamon or vanilla
  (as desired)
8 slices of stale bread
2 peaches
6 apricots
120 g (4.2 oz/generous
  ½ cup) granulated sugar
1 sprig of rosemary
70 g (2.5 oz/⅓ cup)
  village butter (or butter)

4 SERVINGS

For the eggy toast

I beat the milk, the granulated sugar and the eggs
in a large bowl and I add a pinch of cinnamon or
vanilla to season it. I dip the stale bread into the
mixture and wait 5 minutes. Sometimes I use cream
instead of milk for a tastier but richer option.

For the fruit sauté

I peel and slice the peaches. I halve the apricots
and remove their seeds. I sauté the fruit, granulated
sugar and rosemary in 50 g (1.75 oz/½ stick) of
melted butter in a non-stick pan.

In a separate pan, I fry the eggy bread on medium
heat in the remaining 20 g (¾ oz/1 heaped tbsp)
of butter.

Preparing the plate

I place the toast on a long plate, each piece slightly
overlapping the next, and I serve with the sautéed
fruit on top.

Hellim peyniri shish kebab with tomatoes and red onions

250 g (9 oz) *hellim peyniri* *
   (or halloumi)
2 tomatoes
2 red onions
Sea salt
Freshly ground black pepper
A handful of fresh basil
1 clove of garlic
100 ml (3.5 fl oz/scant
   ½ cup) olive oil

4-6 SERVINGS

It is vital for this recipe that all the ingredients are the same size. If they are not, the cheese and the vegetables will cook unevenly. Also, before cooking, I soak thin wooden shish kebab skewers in water for 1 hour to prevent them from burning on the grill.

Hellim peyniri * (or halloumi) is salty, so it is worth tasting it first and, if you find it too salty, soaking it in water before using it.

I dice the *hellim peyniri*, tomatoes and red onions into 1-cm (½-in) cubes and I season the vegetables with sea salt and freshly ground black pepper. Then I place cheese, tomatoes and onion in that order, twice, on each skewer. You may also put tomatoes, cheese or onion by themselves on separate skewers. I place them on a very hot grill and cook until both sides are thoroughly browned—about 3 minutes. I mix basil, garlic and olive oil in a food processor to make a marinade. I place the shish kebab on a plate and drizzle them with marinade.

Preparing the plate

You can make *hellim peyniri* salad by placing the shish kebab on top of a salad or you can serve the them in a shallow dish as a cocktail snack.

* *white, hard, layered goat's or sheep's milk cheese*

Baked red pepper stuffed with *tulum peyniri* and pine nuts

8 red peppers
80 ml (2.7 fl oz/⅓ cup)
   olive oil
Salt
2 cloves of garlic
2 sprigs of rosemary
Freshly ground black pepper
120 g (4.2 oz) *tulum peyniri* *
   (or emmenthal)
1 bunch of basil (or
   fresh oregano)
100 g (3.5 oz) pine nuts
10 g (¼ oz/1 tbsp) currants
1 clove of garlic

4 SERVINGS

For the red pepper

The best red peppers for this recipe are those grown from the end of June to the middle of September that have ample flesh and thin skins. I place the peppers in an oven dish, drizzle olive oil and sprinkle salt over them. I put peeled and halved garlic cloves on the peppers, add rosemary and freshly ground black pepper, and I cover the dish with foil and bake it for 1 hour at 180°C (350°C/Gas 4).

For the stuffing

I buy *tulum peyniri* * (or emmenthal) made of sheep's and goat's milk from Ula market. It has a pungent taste and aroma that complements the sharpness of the peppers (or use emmenthal as an alternative). You can also use *lor peyniri* ** (or ricotta) instead of *tulum peyniri* if you prefer.

I mix the cheese, finely chopped basil, pine nuts (which I had previously browned), currants and crushed garlic thoroughly in a medium-sized bowl and I add some of the peppers' juice from the cooking to this cheese mixture.

To peel the peppers easily, I wrap them in plastic wrap and let them sweat for 15 minutes. After peeling the peppers, I cut them along one side and remove the seeds, and I then stuff the peppers with the cheese mixture.

Preparing the plate

If I am going to serve red peppers stuffed with *tulum peyniri* as an appetizer, I place them side by side on a long plate. During the summer when it is very hot, I serve them with a side of salad as a light and delicious entrée.

* unpasteurized, soft-ripened goat's/sheep's milk cheese
** soft, uncured cheese

Courgette fritters with cucumber and *süzme* yoghurt sauce

For the fritters

1 kg (2 lb 4 oz) courgettes
(zucchini)
Salt
4 eggs
200 g (7 oz/1 cup) flour
3 g (0.1 oz/scant tsp)
baking powder
150 g (5.5 oz) *beyaz peynir* *
(or feta)
1 bunch of parsley
1 bunch of spring onions
(scallions)
1 bunch of dill
Freshly ground black pepper

For the sauce

2 cucumbers
150 g (5.5 oz) *süzme*
yoghurt ** (or cream
cheese)
½ bunch of fresh mint
Salt
Hazelnut oil for frying

4-6 SERVINGS

I choose the most tender courgettes (zucchini) with the firmest skin for making fritters. I grate them (unpeeled) and put them into a sieve and add salt. Since courgettes (zucchini) have a high water content, I draw the water out of them with the salt before making fritters.

I blend the eggs into the courgettes (zucchini) and add the flour and baking powder. After crumbling the *beyaz peynir* * (or feta), I add it, with the chopped parsley, spring onions (scallions) and dill, to the mixture. I season the whole with freshly ground black pepper and put it in the refrigerator to settle.

For the sauce

I make a sauce by liquifying the cucumbers with a handheld blender and then mixing it with the *süzme* yoghurt. I chop the mint finely and add it to the sauce. Alternatively, you may just put the mint through the blender with the cucumber.

I heat the hazelnut oil to 190°C (375°F), place spoonfuls of the fritter mixture into the oil and deep-fry it until golden brown. I serve the courgette (zucchini) fritters with the *süzme* yoghurt ** (or cream cheese) and cucumber sauce.

It is best to place the fritter mixture into the pan with your hand, using your palm as a spoon and slowly dropping the mixture into the oil. If you are afraid of burning your hands or you don't want to get them messy, I recommend that you use a soup spoon.

cow's milk cheese
** *strained, thickened yoghurt that has been left in a cloth overnight to thicken*

MARMARİS

HAVRAN

ALAÇATI
URLA

TİRE

MİLAS

MUĞLA

YALIKAVAK

ULA

MARMARİS

DATÇA
BOZBURUN

MARMARİS market is one of my favourites. It draws people from the villages of Karacasöğüt and Köyceğiz, cheese-sellers and elderly women who gather herbs on the mountainsides. If you miss the main market, which sprawls through the city centre every Thursday, you can catch the 'lite' version on Sunday. The marketplace is set against a stunning backdrop of mountains, pine forests and villages, which offer respite from the overwhelming, chaotic atmosphere of the city.

I love buying turnip greens, wild parsley, nettles, fennel and spinach from the market in spring. I prepare herbs in virtually every conceivable way—sautéing, boiling, roasting, with yoghurt or vinegar. When morel mushrooms appear, I roast them with wild asparagus and break a few village eggs on top, which makes a light lunch. I'm all for simplicity in the kitchen, which does not mean taking the easy way out, but just the absence of a lot of trappings. Sautéing such a precious mushroom as the morel, complementing it with the slightly bitter flavour of wild asparagus, and adding the taste of small, orange-yolked free-range eggs, gives a dish that is more satisfying than many that require much more effort to prepare.

Among the best-known local items in the market are the fragrant strawberries from Karacasöğüt and Çamlı villages. I make desserts and preserves with these and add them to fruit salads in the height of their season, from the end of April to the middle of June.

In addition to the punnets of strawberries I buy for the restaurant, I take another to feast from until I burst as I walk.

I buy what is in season at the market: in the spring, artichokes, peas and broad beans; in early summer, sour cherries, mulberries; in summer, aubergines (eggplant) and tomatoes; at the end of summer, grapes; and in the autumn, pumpkins, quinces and pomegranates. In winter, when oranges, tangerines, bergamot, lemon, cauliflower, broccoli and celeriac become bountiful, I can't make up my mind which ones to buy.

I love approaching the market early on a summer's morning when the fragrance of tomatoes wafts towards you with every step on the still-deserted streets. There are few scents as beautiful as that of freshly gathered tomatoes. The stallholders' own home-grown flowers and the large loaves of köy ekmeği *(village bread) cannot be left out. The seafood called for in the recipes in this chapter can be gotten from the adjoining fish market and fresh offal can always be found at the nearby butchers' shops.*

Dishes capturing the flavours of Marmaris market

- Coriander and gurnard fishcakes, 202
- Dill and pea puree, 206
- *Köy ekmeği* stuffed with *Çerkez tavuğu* and sun-dried tomatoes, 208
- Green olives stuffed with marinated sea bass, 211
- Char-grilled aubergine filled with roasted bell peppers, 214
- *Kağıt helva* with berries and ice cream, 216
- Crushed *Beyaz peynir* with oregano flowers, 218
- Grilled fillet sautéed with beetroot stalks, 220
- Grilled beef tongue and potato salad with capers, 223
- Sardines wrapped in grape leaves with turnip green pesto and tomato salad with sumac, 226
- Jasmine flower fruit salad, 228

Coriander and gurnard fishcakes

600-800 g (1 lb 5 oz-
  1 lb 12 oz) gurnard
2 litres (68 fl oz/2 quarts)
  water
A few sprigs of parsley
1 onion (or a leek)
1 bay leaves
Black peppercorns
Salt
1 orange
2 spring onions (scallions)
1 bunch of fresh coriander
  (cilantro)
100 g (3.5 oz) breadcrumbs

Mayonnaise ingredients
1 egg yolk
10 g (¼ oz/½ tbsp) mustard
1 clove of garlic
Juice of ½ a lemon
A few drops of Tabasco sauce
Salt
Freshly ground black pepper
250 ml (8.5 fl oz/generous
  1 cup) hazelnut oil

4 SERVINGS

Cooking the fish

Fishcakes are only as tasty as the fish you use and the kind of fish you would use for making soup is ideal for fishcakes. I generally use such white-meat fish as gurnard, large-scaled scorpionfish and black scorpionfish. I boil the fish, so I can also make soup from the resulting stock. Another fish you can use for fishcakes is whiting. While it is not as tasty as the others, it is easily available.

The fish used in this recipe is fast-cooking and it will only taste as good as the liquid it is boiled in. So I must start by adding parsley sprigs, the whole onion, a bay leaf, black peppercorns, salt and the orange that I have divided into 2 to a large saucepan of cold water. I simmer the contents for 15-20 minutes. I drop the fish into this delicious boiling water and cook it for 10-15 minutes. I set aside the cooked fish to cool and then remove the bones and tear the meat into chunks (not completely shredded).

Preparation of home-made mayonnaise

Generally, when making fishcakes, we add egg and oil to hold them together. But with these fishcakes, I use mayonnaise because it gives them a great flavour. While a wire whisk produces the best results, if you want to save your arm or, like me, you are going to make a big batch, an electric whisk is useful.

I begin by putting egg yolk, mustard, crushed garlic, lemon juice, Tabasco sauce, salt and freshly ground black pepper into a deep bowl and I whisk them. I gradually add hazelnut oil, which is preferable to the heavier olive oil, and the consistency of the mayonnaise thickens with every spoonful. It doesn't matter if it becomes too thick as you can thin it out again with fish stock.

>>

Coriander and gurnard fishcakes (continued)

Preparation of the vegetables

I use the white and green parts of the spring onions (scallions). I chop them finely so that they provide flavour without becoming dominant. I love using fresh coriander (cilantro) in this recipe but, as the taste of coriander sold in the market is too intense, you should use it sparingly or substitute dill. Turks are rather conservative when it comes to using fresh coriander (cilantro), however, there is no harm in trying.

Kneading the mixture

When I have prepared all the ingredients, I put the fish, mayonnaise and breadcrumbs on a large plate and combine them. I add the spring onions (scallions) and fresh coriander (cilantro) last and knead them in. Then I form the mixture into palm-sized fishcakes and put them on greaseproof paper.

Cooking the patties

I dust the tops and bottoms of the fishcakes with breadcrumbs before cooking them and fry them in a small amount of olive oil in a non-stick frying pan, browning each side in turn. If I'm going to cook fishcakes I prepared earlier and refrigerated, I warm them for 3-5 minutes in an oven to ensure that their insides become thoroughly cooked.

The main ingredients of this recipe are fish, mayonnaise and breadcrumbs, and to these a variety of spices may be added to get the desired flavour. We have had many excellent results in our kitchen using mustard, turmeric, lemon rind and garlic. You can try raw salmon in this recipe but, because it's raw, it is essential that you bake the fishcakes after them browning on both sides.

Dill and pea puree

1 bunch of spring onions
    (scallions), chopped
1 onion, chopped
1 bay leaf
Olive oil
Salt
1 bunch of dill
Freshly ground black pepper
500 ml (18 fl oz/2¼ cups)
    boiling water
500 g (1 lb 2 oz/generous
    3 cups) peas, podded
½ bunch of mint

To serve
Baguettes (French bread)
Full-fat cow's milk cheese

**Flavours compatible
with peas**

Basil, *beyaz peynir* (or
feta), fresh mint, fish,
garlic, spring onions,
dill and mushrooms

The season for peas
is from the end of
spring until the
middle of summer.

4 SERVINGS

I begin by sautéing the spring onions (scallions)
and the onion, and the bay leaf in a little olive oil
in a saucepan. I cook it on a low heat so the onions
don't brown. Adding salt at this stage will release
the juice of the onion without it changing colour.
I wash half a bunch of dill and I add it, uncut, stems
and all. If the dill is tied with string (not an elastic
band), you can leave the tied end upwards so you
can remove it easily later. I add freshly ground
black pepper and water, bring the mixture to the
boil, and add the peas. I leave the pan uncovered to
keep the peas from becoming dark. Once the peas
are cooked and the water has evaporated, I set the
saucepan in ice water to keep the peas bright green.
I finely chop the remaining half bunch of dill
and the mint. I then remove the dill that I cooked
with the peas and add it to the dill and mint I have
chopped. I take the bay leaf out of the saucepan.
Then I take the entire mixture and puree it with
a handheld blender.

Preparation of the croutons

I cut baguettes (French bread) into very long, thin
slices and heat them in an oven at 150°C (300°F/
Gas 2) until they are crisp. When I want to make
the bread extra tasty, I drizzle olive oil and sprinkle
salt over it.

I present the pureed peas with a topping of a thin
slice of full-fat cow's milk cheese and a drizzle of
early harvest extra-virgin olive oil, along with the
croutons. This puree can be served as an entrée or
an appetizer.

Köy ekmeği stuffed with *Çerkez tavuğu* and sun-dried tomatoes

8 slices of bread

1 kg (2 lb 4 oz) fatty
free-range chicken

1 onion, large

2 bay leaves

1 carrot

1 leek

1 clove

1 sprig of fresh oregano

Salt

Black peppercorn

2.5 litres (84 fl oz/
2½ quarts) water

200 g (7 oz) stale bread
without the crusts,
to make the breadcrumbs

500 g (1 lb 2 oz/generous
4½ cups) walnuts

3 cloves of garlic

60 ml (2 fl oz/¼ cup)
grape vinegar

3-5 sun-dried tomatoes

3 g (0.1 oz/scant tsp)
coriander seeds

2-3 sprigs of fresh coriander

1 litre (34 fl oz/1 quart)
chicken stock

1 *köy ekmeği* * (or flat bread
or pitta)

1 bunch of rocket

8 SERVINGS

Cooking the chicken

While washing the chicken, I ensure that no offal remains inside it because it will alter the colour of the chicken stock. I place the washed chicken into a saucepan and cover it with peeled onion, the bay leaves, carrot, leek, the clove and fresh oregano. I add plenty of salt and throw in black peppercorns. I add just enough water to cover the chicken (more or less 2.5 litres/84 fl oz/2½ quarts, depending on the size of the saucepan and the chicken).

Çerkez tavuğu ** is best made with a fatty chicken; since this recipe doesn't use extra fat, the fattier the chicken, the tastier the dish. I want it to have an intense flavour, so I boil the chicken in less rather than more water.

Preparation of the sauce

While the chicken is boiling, I dry the bread in an oven at 100-120°C (215-250°F) and put it through a blender to make fine breadcrumbs. After baking the walnuts at 150°C (300°F/Gas 2), I crush them in a large pestle and mortar, releasing the oil of the walnut, which adds such a wonderful flavour to the *Çerkez tavuğu* sauce. To intensify the flavour of the spice, I heat the coriander seeds over a low flame. I crush the cloves of garlic with a pinch of salt.

After having prepared all of the ingredients, I inspect the chicken. Most likely it is not yet cooked because free-range chickens are more sinewy than the normal ones. But it is worth the wait because of the better flavour of a free-range bird. A chicken over 1 kilo (2 lb 4 oz) takes nearly 2 hours to cook to the desired consistency.

>>

Köy ekmeği stuffed with *Çerkez tavuğu* and sun-dried tomatoes (continued)

Once cooked, I strain the vegetables from the stock and set the chicken, stock and vegetables aside to cool, having placed the chicken in a container that encourages it to cool.

I pull the cooled chicken apart, taking care to discard the cartilage and skin because they are disturbing in the mouth.

I blend the walnuts, coriander seeds, garlic and breadcrumbs together, add dried tomatoes, fresh coriander (cilantro, if desired) and vinegar, and mix again. I slowly add chicken stock to this paste-like mixture, making sure that it does not become too watery and making just enough to cover the chicken meat. I don't want the sauce to be too thick because I don't want the flavour of the ingredients to overwhelm one another. Remember that the breadcrumbs will continue to absorb the juice of the mixture and, because of this, you can end up with a drier mixture when serving than you had anticipated.

I combine the mixture with the chicken pieces and let it stand so that the flavours permeate the whole dish. Leaving it in the refrigerator for half a day produces good results.

I slice the *köy ekmeği* * (or flat bread or pitta), which is round, into eighths (like a cake) and cut horizontally through each slice to open them up as sandwiches. I toast the slices on both sides and put a large dollop of *Çerkez tavuğu* and a few leaves of rocket in as the sandwich filling.

* village bread a simple flat bread prepared on a hot plate, not baked
** a chicken dish with chopped walnuts and a red pepper sauce

Green olives stuffed with marinated sea bass

300 g (10.5 oz) sea bass tail
⅓ bunch of dill
Juice and grated rind of
    1 lemon
Sea salt
Freshly ground black pepper
500 g (1 lb 2 oz) green olives,
    large, fleshy and hard
Early harvest extra-virgin
    olive oil

4 SERVINGS

When choosing the bass, I make sure that it has shiny, firm skin and clear eyes. For this dish it is especially important because any raw fish we eat must be fresh. The fattier the fish, the better it tastes and the larger the fish, the more suitable it is for eating raw. I use the tail meat of the fish raw to stuff the olives, keeping the thicker and meatier parts that are away from the tail for grilling (broiling).

Preparation of the sauce

I add finely chopped dill to a bowl of grated lemon rind and lemon juice and mix.

>>

MOST APPROPRIATE FISH TO EAT RAW
Leerfish, sea bass, sardines, anchovy (*hamsi*), salmon and northern bluefin tuna.
While these fish have distinct flavours, they are good raw. After completely removing their heads and tails, I place sea salt and lemon sauce on layers of anchovies or sardines in a plastic container, and then refrigerate them for a day. You can eat these anchovies or sardines on salads or as entrées. Leerfish has white meat, so it 'cooks' quickly when cut thin. I prepare it like I do sea bass.
Salmon has a distinct flavour and, whether you dice it finely or slice it thinly, it is very tasty when prepared with the same sauce. I don't like adding lemon to northern bluefin tuna; salt and olive oil are sufficient.
Flat fish like turbot are inappropriate for eating raw. I also don't like using fish with strong flavours for raw-fish dishes.

Green olives stuffed with marinated sea bass (continued)

Preparation of the sea bass

After filleting the fish, I cut very thin diagonal slices off the tail. The thinner and more translucent the slices, the easier they are to eat.

I place the thin bass slices on a plate, making sure that they do not overlap, and I dust them with sea salt and then freshly ground pepper, before drizzling the lemon sauce with dill over the top. The salt and acid in the marinade 'cooks' the raw fish in the 2-3 minutes I leave them for.

Preparation of the olives

I remove the pips (pits) from the olives, stuff them, and put them in a bowl, and drizzle extra-virgin olive oil over them.

Olives stuffed with sea bass makes a light, salty appetizer that is especially good with a drink before summer meals.

Char-grilled aubergine filled with roasted bell peppers

6 red peppers
2 cloves of garlic
Olive oil
Salt
2 sprigs of fresh oregano
4 plump aubergines
(eggplant)
50 g (1.75 oz) pine nuts
100 g (3.5 oz) *köy peyniri* *
(or try fresh buffalo
mozzarella)
Freshly ground black pepper

Flavours compatible with aubergines (eggplant)

Garlic, lemon, crushed sesame seeds, basil, yoghurt, vinegar, tomatoes, cheese, lamb and olive oil

4 SERVINGS

Fleshy red peppers are best for char-grilling. It is necessary to wait until the middle of summer for such peppers, which (happily) is the best season for plump aubergines (eggplant).

The *köy peyniri* * (or buffalo mozzarella) used in this recipe is from goat's milk and it can be diced finely and easily, *hellim peyniri* ** (or halloumi) can also be used.

Roasting the peppers

I combine the peppers, 1 clove of garlic, olive oil, salt and freshly ground pepper and bake the mixture at 180°C (350°F/Gas 4) for 15 minutes covered with foil, and an additional 15 minutes uncovered. After I remove the peppers and garlic from the oven, I cover them with plastic wrap and lay them aside to cool. The trapped moisture and heat from the peppers makes them easier to skin. I put the peeled peppers along with the finely chopped garlic into a jar and add just enough olive oil to cover them. I can use the peppers from the jar whenever I wish.

Preparation of the aubergine (eggplant)

I char-grill the aubergine (eggplant) over charcoal, though you may use whatever suitable heat source available to you. A coal fire gives the aubergine (eggplant) a smoky aroma. I hollow out the aubergines (eggplant) carefully and I mix the removed flesh with 1 clove of crushed garlic, olive oil and salt. I cut the prepared peppers into long, thin slices, I sauté the pine nuts in a non-stick pan, and I crumble the cheese with finely chopped fresh oregano. I mix all of these ingredients together and I fill the aubergine (eggplant) shells and bake them at 180°C (350°F/Gas 4) for 10 minutes.

* *village cheese, a fresh, semi-soft and not very salty cheese from cow's/goat's milk*
** *white, hard, layered goat's or sheep's milk cheese*

Kağıt helva with berries and vanilla ice cream

100 g (3.5 oz) strawberries, small, for the sauce

50 g (1.75 oz/¼ cup) caster sugar (superfine sugar)

3 sprigs of basil

½ a lemon

2 *kağıt helva* * (or thin wafers)

250 g (9 oz) strawberries, to place between the wafers

100 g (3.5 oz) mulberries

200 g (7 oz) vanilla ice cream

2 SERVINGS

Preparation of the sauce

I mix the fresh strawberries, caster sugar (superfine sugar), basil leaves and the lemon juice to make a sauce. Because this sauce is very fresh, I prefer it to cooked strawberry sauce. However, if you want to make extra and use it later, you can double the amount of sugar and boil the mixture with lemon juice for 10-15 minutes, before blending it. I do not put basil leaf in cooked strawberry sauce.

It's easy to prepare this dessert. I divide the *kağıt helva** (or thin wafers) into 4 and cut the strawberries in half. To keep the *kağıt helva* from sliding, I place 1 or 2 drops of strawberry sauce in the middle of the plate. I put strawberry sauce on top of the first piece of *helva* and then I add a scoop of vanilla ice cream on top of that. I sprinkle half of the mulberries and strawberries on the ice cream and make a sandwich with another other piece of *kağıt helva* on top and dribble the remaining fruit, ice cream and strawberry sauce over it all.

When I make this for myself, I love separating the layers of *kağıt helva*, making them even thinner.

You can also make this dessert as individual portions or as one large 'cake'. In addition to the mulberries and strawberries, you can use other soft fruits such as blackberries and redcurrants. You can also try apricots and peaches in season.

One of my favourite mixtures is fruit and herbs: strawberry and blackberry, basil and mint; and apricot and peaches, rosemary and fresh oregano. Together, these flavours become intensified. Just as with strawberries, sauces made of raw peach or apricot give the dish a fresh flavour that cooked fruit cannot attain.

* traditional, small-plate-sized, light, sweet wafer

Crushed *beyaz peynir* with oregano flowers

1 kg Ezine *beyaz peynir* *
  (or feta)
1 lemon
100 ml (3.5 fl oz/scant
  ½ cup) early harvest
  extra-virgin olive oil
20 g (0.7 oz) oregano flowers
Freshly ground black pepper
1 *köy ekmeği* ** (or flat bread
  or pitta)
50 ml (2 fl oz/scant ¼ cup)
  olive oil
2 sprigs of rosemary

8 SERVINGS

This recipe is actually my grandfather's. It was my morning breakfast when I was a child. I sometimes serve it as an appetizer with croutons at our restaurant, or as a snack we add to our picnic basket.

I mash the *beyaz peynir** (or feta) in a large bowl with a fork, add some lemon juice and continue mashing. Then I add early harvest extra-virgin olive oil, finely chopped fresh oregano flowers and freshly ground black pepper, and mix it together. I put this mixture into a glass and put a few oregano flowers on top.

I place long, thin slices of *köy ekmeği* ** (or flat bread or pitta) in a large bowl and pour olive oil over them, and sprinkle finely chopped rosemary over all. After ensuring that the bread slices are thoroughly covered and permeated with the olive oil and rosemary, I bake the bread on an oven tray at 150°C (300°F/Gas 2) until it is crispy, for 15-20 minutes. Temperature controls on ovens vary, so keep your eye on the bread.

I put the baked bread strips into a basket and serve them with the *beyaz peynir* puree.

You can make a delicious dressing for green salads by reducing the quantity of cheese and increasing the amount of olive oil and lemon.

* *70% sheep's, 20% cow's, 10% goat's milk cheese local to Ezine in Marmara region of Turkey*
** *village bread a simple flat bread prepared on a hot plate, not baked*

Grilled fillet sautéed with beetroot stalks

For the meat

2 kg (4 lb 8 oz) fillet
(1 whole piece)
Rosemary
Sea salt
Freshly ground black pepper
Olive oil

For the beetroots

2 bunches of beetroot (beets)
stalks
1 clove of garlic
Olive oil
Salt

6 SERVINGS

When I buy fillet, I take care to buy it as one whole piece. The smaller the fillet, the smaller its diameter will be, which makes it difficult to get the results we want. Ask your butcher to remove the sinew from the fillet and, without having anything else done, have it wrapped and leave. You can prepare the fillet in your own kitchen. Cut off and set aside the thin tip and plump section at the top of the fillet. Cut the remaining block of meat into pieces 4-fingers wide, making each piece about 200 g (7 oz). I prepare 180-200-g (6.3-7-oz) portions in the restaurant and this weight is actually the world standard.

I like the fillet to be like a ball and rare and juicy inside, so I prefer the pieces thick, but you can cut thinner slices if you wish to. I leave the pieces to marinate in a relatively flat container, having sprinkled them with freshly ground black pepper, added sprigs of rosemary and some olive oil. You can refrigerate the fillet for a few days like this. It is important not to add salt to this marinade as it will leach out the meat juices, making the final dish less savoury. I prefer adding salt last, just before grilling (broiling) the fillet.

You can marinate the top and tip of the fillet in the same mixture and use them, too. After cooking them in a non-stick pan, you can put the thinly sliced meat into a sandwich or wrap it with thin flatbread. You can also dice the top and tail parts and sauté them in garlic, hot pepper and a little butter.

>>

Grilled fillet sautéed with beetroot stalks (continued)

Cooking the fillet

The grill (or broiler element) should be very hot so that the meat cooks quickly before it releases its juices and becomes like boiled meat. I remove the excess fat from the meat just before cooking it so that it does not cause the charcoal to flame. I salt the meat and place it on a very hot clean grill. For medium-rare meat, I cook both sides for 8-10 minutes each. The best (though slightly risky) way of determining how much the meat has cooked is to press the meat with your finger. Meat toughens as it cooks. So, the greater the indentation made by your finger, the less the meat is cooked.

Preparation of the beetroot stalks

The best way to prepare beetroot (beets) stalks is to steam them. When you cannot find beetroot (beets) stalks, you can use chard or spinach. I like using beetroot (beets) stalks because of their sweetness, so I recommend using them when you can find them. After cooking one side of the fillet and turning it over, I raise the heat and add olive oil. Then I add the beetroot (beets) stalks and sauté them.

If I add salt right at the beginning, the water in the stems will be released and hamper the sautéing. Also, if you add garlic at the beginning, by the time the beetroot (beets) stalks are ready, the garlic will have burned. Therefore, I add the salt and crushed garlic last, turn the meat over a few times and then put it on a plate with the sautéed beetroot (beets) stalks as a side.

Grilled beef tongue and potato salad with capers

1 whole beef tongue
1.5 litre (51 fl oz/1½ quarts)
    water
1 onion
2 bay leaves
5 black peppercorns
Salt
Olive oil

For the potato salad
1 kg (2 lb 4 oz) fresh
    potatoes, small
A few bay leaves
Salt
1 egg yolk
10 g (¼ oz/½ tbsp)
    mustard
1 clove of garlic
Juice of ½ a lemon
3-5 drops of Tabasco sauce
Freshly ground black pepper
250 ml (8.5 fl oz/generous
    1 cup) hazelnut oil
20 g (0.7 oz) capers
2 sprigs of parsley
Salt

8 SERVINGS

Cooking the tongue

I remove the blood from the tongue by soaking it overnight in salted water. If I am short of time, 1-2 hours is enough, but I change the water every half hour. After removing the tongue from the water, I put it into a big pan with onion, the bay leaves, black peppercorns and salt. I then add water and cook it for 2-2.5 hours or, with a pressure cooker, 1-1.5 hours.

I remove the rough skin of the tongue while it is hot, because if you wait until it has cooled, it won't peel off. I wrap the whole tongue in plastic wrap and throw it into the refrigerator. Tongue that has been in the refrigerator for 1-2 hours can be cut more easily.

Though I'm not using it in this recipe, I never waste the tongue stock. It's ideal for cooking rice. While it may be a bit heavy, I love serving rice made with tongue stock seasoned with plenty of black pepper as a side dish with meat.

>>

For the potato salad

After washing the potatoes, I put them in a large pan. Then I boil them for half an hour with some bay leaves, salt and plenty of water on medium heat. The cooking time of a potato changes depending on its kind, but you can test whether it is done but poking a knife or wooden skewer into the potato.

I mix egg yolk, mustard, crushed garlic, lemon juice, Tabasco sauce, salt and freshly ground black pepper in a deep bowl with an electric beater. I gradually add hazelnut oil and I fold capers into what is now a liquid mayonnaise. After adding chopped parsley, I mix it all well, add the potatoes while they are still warm and cover them thoroughly.

Warm potatoes help the flavours to blend into one another. It doesn't matter if you use olive oil-lemon dressing, mayonnaise or yoghurt; just make sure that the potatoes you use in any kind of potato salad are not cold. Also, remember to prepare twice as much dressing as you would use in a normal salad because potatoes are a starchy food and so absorb a lot of dressing.

Grilling (broiling)

I remove the tongue from the refrigerator and cut it into 1-cm (½-in)-thick slices. I cover the slices with a little olive oil, sprinkle freshly ground black pepper, and cook each side for 1 minute on a very hot grill. The outside of the tongue should be crispy but the inside should melt in your mouth.

Preparing the plate

I place 2 tongue slices in the middle of the plate and serve it with potato salad as a side.

Sardines wrapped in grape leaves with turnip green pesto and tomato salad with sumac

**For the sardines wrapped
   in grape leaves**

24 sardines
12 fresh grape leaves
Salt
Olive oil
Freshly ground black pepper

For the turnip green pesto

1 bunch of turnip greens
Salt
2 cloves of garlic
100 g (3.5 oz) pine nuts
Extra-virgin olive oil

**For the tomato salad
   with sumac**

2 tomatoes
1 cucumber
1 red onion
1 lemon
Extra-virgin olive oil
Sumac (or lemon zest)
2 sprigs of parsley

4 SERVINGS

Sardines are found in the Marmara, Aegean and Mediterranean seas. While they are available all year round in the Marmara, the tastiest ones are caught in the Aegean and the Mediterranean at the end of July and August. Fish during this season have more scales and are fattier, making them ideal for grilling (broiling).

Sardines in grape leaves

I remove the bones and heads from the sardines and then place two fish in the middle of each grape leaf. I put a pinch of salt and olive oil over the top. After adding freshly ground black pepper, I roll the grape leaves into flattened, closed tubes. Once I have finished preparing all the other ingredients I am going to use, I grill (broil) the sardine roll over charcoal and cook them on both sides for about 2-4 minutes each side.

Turnip green pesto

I add a pinch of salt to boiling water and boil the turnip greens for 10 minutes. Then I put them in cold or icy water to stop the cooking and to help them retain their greenness. I shake the turnip greens well after removing them from the water.

I blend the turnip greens, garlic and sautéed pine nuts in a blender. Gradually adding olive oil, I bring the mixture to the consistency of a thin sauce. The tartness of the turnip and the garlic go well with the sardines wrapped in grape leaves.

Tomato salad

I dice the seedless and firm part of the tomato, cucumber and red onion into 0.5-cm (¼-in) cubes and mix them with lemon juice, olive oil, sumac (or lemon zest) and parsley.

Preparing the plate

I place the sardines on a long plate and put the turnip green pesto over the top, and serve with the tomato salad in a separate bowl.

Jasmine flower fruit salad

500 g (1 lb 2 oz/2½ cups)
  sugar
500 ml (18 fl oz/2¼ cups)
  water
Juice of ½ lemon
1 handful of jasmine flowers
100 g (3.5 oz) strawberries
1 green apple
1 orange
1 large pear
100 g (3.5 oz) sour cherries

4 SERVINGS

We use jasmine in this recipe but I also love using orange flower or lavender, depending on the season. Orange flowers begin blooming in late spring and bear fruit at the beginning of summer. They have a strong scent. So, during this season, orange gardens and the surrounding streets have a rich fragrance of flowers. I like capturing this intense, sweet fragrance in syrup and using it in desserts.

For the syrup

I put sugar and water into a pan, add the juice of half a lemon and mix. Once the sugar has melted, I add a handful of jasmine flowers and simmer the whole mixture. After about 15 minutes, when it has reached the consistency of syrup, I set it aside.

For the fruit salad

I cut the strawberries into halves and dice the unpeeled green apple. I divide the orange into segments. To do this, I top and tail the orange, place it on a cutting board, and cut the skin from top to bottom. Then I slice the skinless orange so that the threads of pith cannot be seen. I dice the pear, remove the pips from the sour cherries, and mix all of the ingredients together. Finally, I drizzle 1 soup spoon of jasmine flower syrup into the mixture.

I like the jasmine aroma to have a strong presence, but by adjusting the amount of syrup you add, you can get the sweetness and aroma you desire.

You can use various fruits in the fruit salad, depending on the season. I don't recommend bananas because they darken, but fruit like blackberries, mulberries or grapes go well in salad.

BOZBURUN

HAVRAN

ALAÇATI
URLA

TİRE

MİLAS

MUĞLA

YALIKAVAK
ULA

MARMARİS

DATÇA
BOZBURUN

*T*O REACH the Bozburun Peninsula, I usually take the İçmeler-Turunç road. I spend a great portion of the year on this peninsula and I encounter a wide variety of natural colours and scents whenever I walk along its narrow forest paths. Spring cedes to summer, daisies and poppies gradually give way to pink oleanders. In the springtime, almonds are my favourite trees and, in the summertime, walnuts. I love roaming the magnificent pine forests and exploring the bays and coves of turquoise water in the spring.

Bayır village is distinctive for its coffee house shaded by a centuries-old plane tree. The stone houses, constructed on terraces, hint at the village's ancient roots. Touristic though it now is, the village has not lost its charm. I leave the village and follow the signs for Söğüt, a small coastal settlement. In stark contrast to the forests inland, this side of the peninsula is barren. I am fascinated by the change of textures between places that are only half an hour apart. A few buildings, a handful of small boats on the shore, and a clutch of bed-and-breakfasts and fish restaurants are all there is. Sailing from bay to bay in the height of summer, onshore I see healthy, smiling children lining the roads to sell figs: first, ripe green ones and later, in August, black or purple ones with honey-coloured flesh. In the autumn, they are sold dried.

I reach Bozburun, pass its boatyard and enter this small town to see Symi Island on the horizon—and a wonderful sunset. Bozburun's fishmongers are the ideal source for the seafood needed for the *recipes I will now share with you. The seasonal fish and other seafood are so fresh that they smell of iodine. Despite their freshness, in extremely hot weather, the wise shop early.*

Approaching Selimiye, my eye is drawn to a small island and the old fortress in the middle of the cove. I see small shops lining both sides of the road displaying signs advertising elma yağı *(apple oil). In fact, this oil is extracted from sage seeds, which resemble apple seeds. I come across fresh oregano, sage and myrtle around the coves.*

The main source of income in the area is apiculture. In the interior of the peninsula and at higher elevations, particularly at Osmaniye village, honey is produced in the pine forests. At the end of summer and into October, it is possible to find fresh pine honey.

Orhaniye, in marked contrast to the openness of the coastal settlements, is located up a sheltered inlet, creating a positive, sheltered environment away from sea breezes. The motionless water adds to the timeless atmosphere.

*After the spring and autumn rains, the villagers collect red pine mushrooms (*Lactarius deliciosus, *also known as saffron milk-cap or, simply, pine mushrooms, and* çıntar *in Turkish), a species that thrives in pine forests, and morel mushrooms (*Morchella esculenta, *locally known as* kuzu göbeği, *or lamb's belly, mushrooms). Grilled pine mushrooms and sautéed morels are delicious.*

Dishes capturing the flavours of Bozburun market

- White grouper with samphire sautéed with garlic and lemon peel, 234
- Baked figs stuffed with honey and almonds served with warm goat's cheese, 238
- Grilled squid with white cheese and char-grilled aubergine stuffing, 240
- *Köy eriştesi* with sage, walnut and white cheese, 244
- Grilled crayfish with olive oil, rocket and parsley dressing, 246
- Courgette, green apple, dill, fresh mint and *lor peyniri* salad , 248
- Bread rolls baked in a wood-fired oven, 250

White grouper with samphire sautéed with garlic and lemon peel

4 SERVINGS

For the grouper

1½-2 kg (3 lb 5 oz-4 lb 8 oz)
   white grouper (or grouper
   or halibut)
Sea salt
Freshly ground black pepper
Early harvest extra-
   virgin olive oil
1 spring onion (scallion)
1 clove of garlic
Juice of ½ an orange
2 lemons

For the samphire

3 bunches of samphire
1 clove of garlic
½ a lemon
Extra-virgin olive oil
Freshly ground black pepper
50 g (1.75 oz) breadcrumbs
   (see box, p. 236)

The small fishing boats and the fishmongers that line the Bozburun coast are ideal sources for the catch of the day. Despite a summertime commercial fishing ban, it is easy to catch grouper using a rod and line. Unlike many other types of fish found in Turkish waters, grouper is available throughout the year. Because it has white flesh, it contains less fat compared with darker-fleshed fish and it has a lighter taste. White-fleshed fish are also easier to digest, so they can be eaten easily on hot summer days. Grouper is caught off Turkey's Aegean and Mediterranean shores.

HOW TO BUY FRESH FISH

When choosing fish, I make sure that the eyes are bright and convex. Fresh fish also have bright, taut skin. As scale-less fish start to decay, the brightness of their skin fades and wrinkles emerge, particularly on the belly. Fresh scaled fish have firmly attached scales. Do not be fooled by how bright the fish looks because the fishmongers continuously sprinkle the fish with water to make them look attractive. Another way to gauge if fish is fresh is to hold it by its head, tail up. If the tail remains upright, the fish is fresh; if the tail droops, it isn't. Also, the gills of fresh fish are vivid red.

For the samphire

I begin by washing the samphire thoroughly. I boil water in a large saucepan and add the samphire. Naturally salty, there is no need to add salt when boiling samphire. I cook it for about 20 minutes until I can easily detach it from its stem. I put the cooked samphire in chilled water to halt the cooking process and ensure that it keeps its green colour.

Samphire is a summer plant, most abundant from June to September, though you can also find it in the spring.

I chop the garlic finely and I take the peel of half a lemon and cut it into thin, lengthwise strips. I pour some olive oil into a preheated pan on high heat and add the drained samphire.

White grouper with samphire sautéed with garlic and lemon peel (continued)

⁓⌾⁓

FOR THE BREADCRUMBS
Ready-made breadcrumbs are a convenient
alternative, though I prefer to make my own.
I put a quarter loaf of bread in an oven preheated to
150ºC (300ºF/Gas 2) and leave it for 10-15 minutes
until it becomes fairly hard. The easiest way to turn
the cooled bread into crumbs is to use a blender.
For a crispy texture, the samphire can be
served immediately after mixing it with the
breadcrumbs. Alternatively, you can leave the
mixture standing so that the breadcrumbs soften as
they absorb the garlic and samphire juices,
amplifying their flavours.

⁓⌾⁓

I add the lemon peel and sauté it for 3-5 minutes
and then I add the chopped garlic and stir a couple
of times (if you add the garlic first, it burns before
the samphire and lemon peel is ready, leaving
a bitter taste). Finally, I add the freshly ground
pepper and the breadcrumbs and I stir them in
before plating. You can also substitute chopped
almonds for the breadcrumbs. If you prepare the
same dish towards the end of the summer, as the
weather gets cooler, you can use butter instead
of olive oil for a deeper flavour.

For the grouper

I de-scale and fillet the grouper (or halibut). After
removing any remaining large bones with tweezers,
and leaving the skin on, I divide the fish into
200-g (7-oz) portions (keeping the head and the
bones of the grouper for fish soup). When I cook
for the family, I generally don't remove the bones
that remain after filleting although it would not
enhance a restaurant's reputation if guests find
too many bones.

White grouper with samphire sautéed with garlic and lemon peel (continued)

Flavours that complement white grouper

Almond, bay leaves, cucumber, lemon, olive oil, garlic, tomato, fresh oregano, sea salt, black olive, watercress, rocket and dill

A versatile fish, white grouper can be baked, smoked, grilled or steamed.

After sprinkling a pinch of salt and freshly ground black pepper on the fillets, I coat them with olive oil. The best cooking method to ensure delicious results is char-grilling.

We use a large barbecue in our kitchen. I burn the charcoal to embers before I start cooking and I ensure that the charcoal I buy is not just dust but firm pieces, preferably from oak. When the embers are ready, I heat the cooking grate and then clean it using a grate brush or half an onion on the end of a fork. Make sure whatever you put on the grate is not too oily as the oil will burn, leaving an unpleasant smoky smell and bitter taste on the food.

I place the grouper fillets skin-side down on the grate and I turn them over when the skin is branded. I make sure that fish fillets remain juicy by cooking them on each side for 5-8 minutes. While the fish is cooking, I cut the lemons in half and place them open-side down next to the fillets and cook them until they are branded.

Seafood tastes great if it is marinated after cooking and you can prepare the marinade while the food is cooking. I place thinly sliced spring onion (scallion) in a dish that is not too deep but can hold the fillets comfortably. I crush and add garlic and squeeze the juice from half an orange and mix everything together thoroughly. Finally, I slowly pour in the olive oil, and then I remove the cooked grouper fillets from the barbecue, and marinate them before serving.

Presentation

I place the samphire in the middle of warmed service plates. I then place the grouper on top, garnish with a grilled half lemon at the side and serve.

Baked figs stuffed with honey and almonds served with warm goat's cheese

8 figs

2 sprigs of rosemary

100 g (3.5 oz/scant 1 cup) fresh almonds

100 g (3.5 oz/generous ¼ cup) Marmaris pine honey (see box)

300 g (10.5 oz) soft goat's cheese

10 g (¼ oz/1½ tsp) pine honey for drizzling

4 SERVINGS

The sweetness and smell of figs and pine honey balance the strong flavour of goat's cheese. Fresh goat's cheese has a short storage life so you should consume it within a few days of buying it. When I can't find fresh goat's cheese, I use hard village cheese made from goat's milk. Village cheese is lightly salted, so it complements the figs and the honey well.

I can also find carob honey, flower honey and blended honeys and I use these to come up with different flavours.

For the baked figs

I slice the figs in half. I chop the rosemary leaves. I roast the almonds for about 10 minutes in an oven preheated to 150ºC (300ºF/Gas 2) and, after cooling them, I crush them, taking care not to break them up too much. If I prefer to have larger almond pieces, I chop them with a sharp knife instead. I mix the almonds with the honey and rosemary and put this mixture on the upward-facing open side of each half fig. You can also use quince or pear in instead of figs. For the best results, cut the quince or pears in 2, remove the seeds and fill them with the almond stuffing and bake them. Figs, however, absorb the stuffing's flavour much better than the other fruits do.

I place the stuffed figs on greaseproof paper on a tray and bake them for 10-15 minutes in an oven preheated to 180ºC (350ºF/Gas 4).

Presentation

I slice the fresh goat's cheese into 0.5-cm (¼-in) widths, each slice big enough to cover the figs. I flatten the figs slightly and place the goat's cheese on top and return them to the oven. Once the cheese is soft and browned on top, I place the figs side by side on plates and drizzle honey over them and serve.

PINE HONEY

Pine honey is unique in that, unlike other honey types, it is produced by bees that process resin from pine bark rather than flower nectar. Produced in the warmer months, this opaque brown honey has a distinctive sharp taste and it is resistant to crystallization. Pine honey is only available in Turkey and Greece. I try to ensure that the honey is stored in a dry, cool environment. The ideal location is a dark cupboard away from heat sources such as ovens and refrigerators.

Grilled squid with white cheese and char-grilled aubergine stuffing

4 SERVINGS

½ kg (1 lb 2 oz) squid
(8-10 pieces)
1 spring onion (scallion)
1-2 cloves garlic
Albanian pepper (or red
pepper flakes)
Extra-virgin olive oil

For the stuffing

2 aubergines (eggplant)
200 g (7 oz) white cheese,
preferably from Ezine
in western Turkey (or feta)
1 clove of garlic
Early harvest extra-
virgin olive oil
1 bunch of fresh basil

For serving

2 bunches of cress
½ a lemon
Early harvest extra
virgin olive oil
Sea salt

For the stuffing

The best season for aubergine (eggplant) is June to September. When choosing an aubergine (eggplant), I make sure that it is dark-purple, the skin is firm, and that they are white at the bottom rather than green, which indicates a bitter taste. Aubergines (eggplant) contain a lot of moisture, so before I cook them, I prick them to prevent them from bursting. Then I char-grill them on a griddle or barbecue, or over a naked flame. I grill (broil) the aubergine (eggplant) until they become soft inside, the skins appear empty, and they smell smoked. You shouldn't take the aubergine (eggplant) from the heat too early as undercooked aubergine (eggplant) tastes bitter. Grilling (broiling) time for aubergine (eggplant) depends on size, but usually takes 10-15 minutes.

I peel the cooked aubergines (eggplant) while they are hot and I mash them. I mix in white cheese (or feta), add crushed garlic, olive oil and finely chopped basil.

For the squid

I first remove the outer membrane of the squid. There is a quill that runs the inside the length of the body tube of the squid and this is connected to its ink sacks. With the squid immersed in a bowl of water, I put my fingers inside the tube and gently pull out the quill, while being careful not to burst the ink sacks, which can be messy. The quill also comes out with the head and tentacles. I consider the tentacles more delicious than the tube, so I cut them off the head just under the eyes and I throw the quill, ink sacks and head away. (You can ask a fishmonger to do this for you.)

The secret of this recipe is to marinate the squid well. I use thinly sliced spring onion (scallion), peeled garlic, Albanian pepper (or red pepper flakes) and extra-virgin olive oil for the marinade and leave the squid in it for a day in the refrigerator. Most fish restaurants tenderize squid by kneading it in mineral water with salt and sugar for 5-10 minutes, but this is unnecessary for small fresh squid.

>>

Grilled squid with white cheese and char-grilled aubergine stuffing (continued)

I stuff the marinated squid tubes with the aubergine (eggplant) and white cheese stuffing and close the end with a toothpick. I cook each side of the squid for 3 minutes on a preheated grill (or under a broiler).

Squid can become rubbery while cooking because it contains a lot of muscle and collagen. To avoid this, it has to be grilled either for no more than 3-5 minutes or for over an hour. So, I make sure I don't overcook squid, grilling the tentacles and the tube for only a short time. You can place the tentacles on the grill later than the tubes because they cook faster.

Preparing the plates

I add lemon juice, olive oil and sea salt to the washed and dried cress. I place a few bunches of cress on each plate and I place the stuffed squid hot from the grill alongside and I serve after removing the toothpicks.

Köy eriştesi with sage, walnut and white cheese

2 litres (68 fl oz/ 2 quarts)
    water
200 g (7 oz) thinly sliced
    köy eriştesi * (or noodles)
Salt
50 g (1.75 oz/½ stick) butter
50 g (1.75 oz/scant ½ cup)
    chopped walnuts
1 bunch of sage
1 bunch of fresh oregano
1 sprig of parsley
1 clove of garlic
100 g (3.5 oz) white cheese
    (or feta)
Salt
Freshly ground black pepper

4 SERVINGS

I boil the water in a large pan and add a pinch of salt. If you add salt to the cool water, it takes longer to boil. After adding the *köy eriştesi* * (or noodles), I stir it for a few minutes to prevent it from sticking and I let it cook for 5-7 minutes with the lid off. Before draining the *köy eriştesi*, I draw off a glass of boiling water and leave it aside.

The full pleasure of pasta and noodles comes when it can slide smoothly down your throat. Usually this is attained by using tomato sauce or cream, but the same perfection can be achieved by adding boiling water, in addition to butter and olive oil to the pasta.

After putting the *köy eriştesi* aside, I roast the chopped walnuts in butter on a low heat. After the walnuts begin to brown, I add the sage leaves and garlic and then the boiling water I kept aside. Then I add the *köy eriştesi* and stir.

I chop the oregano and parsley finely. I crumble the white cheese (or feta) and add it to the *köy eriştesi* together with the oregano and parsley. If I cook this dish for myself, I also sprinkle freshly ground black pepper liberally over the top.

* *home-made noodles*

Grilled crayfish with olive oil, rocket and parsley dressing

2 crayfish, 500-600 g
   (1 lb 2 oz-1 lb 5 oz) each
½ an orange
10-15 sprigs of parsley
250 ml (8.5 fl oz/generous
   1 cup) white wine
10 black pepper seeds
Salt

For the dressing
1 bunch of rocket
½ a bunch of parsley
1 clove of garlic
1-2 drops of lemon juice
Sea salt
Freshly ground pepper
Early harvest extra-virgin oil

4 SERVINGS

For the crayfish

Cooking crayfish is not as scary as you may think.
All you need is a large pan and a few other items.

I put some cold water in the pan and add orange,
parsley sprigs, white wine, black pepper seed, salt
and the crayfish. I close the lid and leave it to cook.
After the water starts boiling, I turn off the heat
and leave the crayfish in the boiled water for
another 5 minutes.

After the crayfish is cooked, I divide it in 2 and
dress it with olive oil. I prepare the grill, see
p. 237 for information on how to do this). I cook
the crayfish until it is branded by the grill and
then I place the crayfish on a plate.

Make sure that crustaceans such as crayfish and
lobster are alive when you purchase them.

The cooking method I explained above seems the
most humane. The alternative of throwing a live
crayfish into water that is already boiling causes
the animal to 'scream', which can be distressing for
the cook, not to mention the crayfish. If you choose
this method, I suggest you pull the crayfishes'
heads off to prevent them suffering. Even with the
heads off, the insides of the crayfish will not come
out. If you prefer this method, after you have boiled
the crayfish for 5 minutes, you should immerse it in
iced water. Even though this method is superior in
terms of temperature and cooking control, it feels
inhumane because of the way the crayfish dies. So,
I recommend the first method I described.

How to increase the flavour of crayfish

I chop the rocket, parsley, garlic and lemon juice
in a blender and then I pour it into a small cup, add
salt and black pepper and stir the mixture slowly
while adding olive oil. I then pour the mixture over
the crayfish and serve it.

Courgette, green apple, dill, fresh mint and *lor peyniri* salad

2 green courgettes (zucchini)
1 green apple
½ a bunch of dill
1 spring onion (scallion)
150 g (5.5 oz) *lor peyniri* *
    (or ricotta)
20 g (¾ oz/1 heaped tbsp)
    black cumin (optional)
100 ml (3.5 fl oz/scant
    ½ cup) vinegar
Sea salt
Freshly ground black pepper
Juice of ½ a lemon
Early harvest extra-
    virgin olive oil

4 SERVINGS

I slice the courgette (zucchini) and apple as thinly as possible (a commercial slicing machine is ideal for attaining ultra-thin slices). I put the apple slices in water with lemon to prevent them from darkening.

I tear off and finely chop the dill. I also finely chop the spring onion (scallion) and mix it with the courgette (zucchini), dill, apple, *lor peyniri* * (or ricotta) and black cumin. I add vinegar and then salt and, finally, olive oil and mix them. If you add the olive oil first, the salad won't absorb the vinegar.

I place the salad in the middle of a large salad plate or spread it on a long plate. Then I serve.

Instead of *lor peyniri* you can use Erzincan *tulum peyniri* ** (or fontina) or goat's cheese. Erzincan *tulum peyniri* is salty and has a sharp flavour, so you should salt the salad sparingly. If you can't find ball-shaped green courgettes (zucchini), you can make this salad by cutting normal courgettes (zucchini) longitudinally. If you use green and yellow courgettes (zucchini) together, your salad will be more colourful.

* *soft, uncured cheese*
** *unpasteurized, soft-ripened goat's milk cheese local*
    to Erzincan in Anatolia, Turkey

Bread rolls baked in a wood-fired oven

40 g (1.4 oz) wet (fresh) yeast
450 ml (15 fl oz/scant
    2 cups) water
1 kg (2 lb 4 oz/8 cups) flour
100 g (3.5 oz/scant ½ cup)
    salt
25 g (1 oz) granulated sugar
125 ml (4.4 fl oz/generous
    ½ cup) hazelnut oil

For the glaze
2 egg yolks
50 g (1.75 oz) yoghurt
50 g (1.75 oz) sesame seeds

18 SERVINGS

I mix the wet (fresh) yeast with 100 ml (3.5 fl oz/scant ½ cup) warm water and leave it to stand for 10 minutes. I pour the flour onto a work surface and make a crater in the middle of it, into which I put the salt and the sugar. Then I add the oil, wet yeast and 225 ml (7.6 fl oz/scant 1 cup) water and start kneading. I add the remaining water slowly as I continue kneading.

When the dough reaches a soft, non-sticky consistency, I put it in a bowl and leave it to prove for 30 minutes with a tea towel over the top. Then I knead the dough again and divide it into approximately 18 lemon-size rolls and place them in rows on an oven tray. After leaving them to rest under a cloth for 15 minutes, I flatten the rolls.

I mix the yoghurt and egg yolk in a cup and I brush this mixture on the rolls. Then I sprinkle black sesame seeds on top.

I place the tray in a wood oven preheated to 150°C (300°F/Gas 2). After 5-7 minutes, great-smelling small puffy rolls are ready to serve. I sometimes prepare round and sometimes elongated rolls.

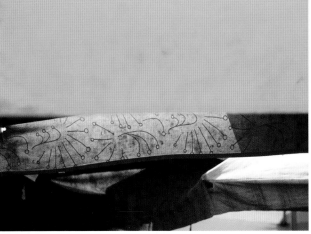

DATÇA

HAVRAN

ALAÇATI
URLA

TİRE

MİLAS

MUĞLA

YALIKAVAK
ULA

MARMARİS

DATÇA
BOZBURUN

I BELIEVE that Datça owes a lot to its unspoilt, winding roads. Being off the beaten track at the far end of a narrow peninsula, no one just passes through Datça; everyone who goes there goes to visit Datça Peninsula. The first words that come to mind when describing this place are 'remote' and 'beautiful'. The journey there, with the Aegean's Gökova Gulf on your right, and the Mediterranean's Hisarönü landscape on your left, is very picturesque. Looking down on Balıkaşıran, the peninsula's narrow waist, you see the two gulfs are separated by just a sliver of land. Along the entire road, there are pine forests and curious red boulders, and, as you approach Datça, the incense (storax) trees and olive groves greet you. The dry and breezy climate here is unique, like so many other things.

Datça's market day is Saturday. To experience all the uniquely seasonal flavours offered at this covered street market, you must visit it at many times of year. This market's most important wares is almonds. The market stalls, filled with green almonds in April, overflow with almonds of all sizes by the end of summer. The most delicious and famous of the almonds grown around Datça is the nurlu (radiant) almond. Though it is pleasant to eat green almonds just dipped in salt, I love them served in olive oil with plenty of herbs.

At the end of May, piles of fresh chickpeas are sold. Those who have only eaten canned or dried chickpeas should really taste them fresh. These green, moist chickpeas, which melt in your mouth, are a delicious snack.

From the middle of July, the stalls turn bright-red with large, meaty Datça tomatoes. With few seeds, these tomatoes add zest to any meal when they are dressed with just salt and olive oil. They are exceptionally delicious and satisfying. Datça tomatoes are at their tastiest in mid-September. At the beginning of summer, I buy pink tomatoes, which are rather delicate and do not like the heat. When buying pink tomatoes, be careful not to crush them or put them on top of one another.

Datça is surrounded by oregano, so the honey sold at the market is oregano honey. Compared with the pine honey in Marmaris, oregano honey is less bitter but its fragrance is stronger. At the end of summer, when honey becomes available, it is also possible to find carob honey in the market.

When I want a refreshing break from my busy schedule, I follow the road signs for Knidos and stop in Palamutbükü, where I take an early morning dip in the turquoise sea, and then I breakfast on menemen, a type of scrambled egg dish with lots of pepper and tomato. With no time to linger, I head off to Datça market for first pick of the produce and to enjoy chatting with the stallholders. Datça market has a festive atmosphere full of conversation and laughter. I love the stallholders' stories. In essence, I take my time to savour every moment and every greeting.

Dishes capturing the flavours of Datça market

- Caramelized sea bass, baked figs and herbs with crushed almond dressing, 256
- Green almonds in olive oil, 259
- Grilled Gökova shrimp with creamed sweetcorn soup, 260
- Casserole of Datça tomatoes, aubergines, *köy peyniri* and fresh herbs, 264
- Aubergine stuffed with stewed lamb, 266
- Fish soup, 268
- Marinated lamb spare ribs, 270
- Pink tomato and *köy ekmeği* salad, 272
- Baked sea bream with capers and olives, 274
- Grilled red mullet and warm cannellini bean puree with lemon rind, 276

Caramelized sea bass, baked figs and herbs with crushed almond dressing

4 SERVINGS

For the sea bass

2 sea bass, about 1 kg
  (2 lb 4 oz) each
Table salt
Freshly ground black pepper
2 pinches of granulated sugar
Olive oil
50 g (1.75 oz/½ stick) butter
4 spring onions (scallions)
4 fresh figs

For the salad

¼ bunch of dill
¼ bunch of parsley
¼ bunch of tarragon
¼ bunch of fresh mint
Juice and rind of 1 lemon
100 g (3.5 oz/scant 1 cup)
  nurlu almonds (or
  almonds)
100 ml (3.5 fl oz/scant ½
  cup) extra-virgin olive oil
Sea salt

Preparation of the sea bass

I have the fishmonger clean and, if possible, de-scale the fish. If I de-scale the fish myself, I hold each one inside a plastic bag in the sink and scrape the scales off with a knife, scraping against the lay of the scales. To successfully fillet the fish, you need a sharp knife so that you can cut into the fish from right under its head. Holding the fish flat on a cutting board, I cut with the knife parallel to the board, and, following the bone, I remove the fillet from the bone. Then I turn the fish over and repeat. Two bass are enough for 4 portions. Because a 1-kilo (2 lb 4 oz) sea bass has thick meat, the fillets don't dry out. I sprinkle salt and freshly ground black pepper on the fillets, first on the exposed white-meat side then on the skin side. I also sprinkle a pinch of sugar on the skin.

Preparation of the figs

After dividing the figs into 2, I sprinkle a pinch of granulated sugar on them, place them on an oven tray and then I bake them at 150°C (300°F/ Gas 2). 10-15 minutes is sufficient to bring the figs to the consistency I want.

SEA BASS

The sea-bass-fishing season is between May and September, but it is also extensively fished in the Aegean in November, December, January and February. Though sea bass can weigh up to 20 kg (44 lb), they are at their most delicious when they weigh between 1.5 and 3 kg (3 lb 5oz and 6 lb 8 oz). Sea bass, which is the mainstay of the dolphin's diet, move from the open sea to the coast, where they prefer shallow, reedy areas. Because they travel in schools, it is possible to catch a lot of them in a short period of time.

>>

Caramelized sea bass, baked figs and herbs with crushed almond dressing (continued)

Preparation of the herb salad

I place the leaves and stalks of dill, parsley, tarragon and fresh mint in a large bowl. I make a thick vinaigrette by blending lemon juice, grated lemon rind, almonds and olive oil with a hand blender and I pour this sauce onto the herbs and mix thoroughly. Finally, I sprinkle sea salt on top.

Cooking the fish

I drizzle olive oil into a large, non-stick frying pan. Once the pan is hot, I begin to sauté the fish, skin-side down, and I reduce the heat to medium. When the skin side has caramelized, I cook the other side and add butter. Once the butter has melted, I tilt the pan and baste the fillets. At the same time, I add whole spring onions (scallions) to the pan. Once the onions have softened, I put the contents of the pan on a wide serving plate, leaving the excess butter in the pan. I place the figs on top of the fish and serve it with the herb salad on the side.

While the dish may seem rich because of the butter, when the bass is cooked this way, its rich taste is balanced by the spring onions (scallions) and the sweet figs. The herbs acquire a pleasant mix of flavours when the aroma of the almonds and the acid of the lemon combine.

This dish is the most popular one at my restaurant along the coast in Kumlubük. Uncertain though my customers may be when, on recommendation, they order this dish for the first time, they later return for it again and again.

Green almonds in olive oil

1 kg (2 lb 4 oz) green
   almonds (see box)
1 onion, large
100 ml (3.5 fl oz/scant
   ½ cup) olive oil
30 g (1 oz) flour
Boiling water
Salt
2 sugar cubes
1 bunch of dill
Freshly ground black pepper

8 SERVINGS

I remove the stems from the green almonds and wash them with plenty of water. I peel the onion and chop it up into small pieces.

I sauté the onions in olive oil in a medium-sized pan over a moderate flame. Then I add the green almonds, sautéing the whole mixture for another 1-2 minutes. I dust the mixture with flour and stir it with a wooden spoon.

I pour boiling water over the green almonds until they are covered. After adding the salt, sugar cubes, half of the dill and the black pepper, I cover the pan and keep it on a low heat until the almonds become very soft. To prevent the almonds turning black after cooking, I stand the pan in a container of icy water.

Once the almonds are cooked, I serve them with a sprinkling of finely chopped dill.

GREEN ALMONDS
In Turkey, green almonds are grown mostly in the Aegean and on the Datça Peninsula. The almond tree originated in central Asia and China. It was brought to Turkey on the Silk Road, and from there it was carried to other Mediterranean countries. The green almond tree now cultivated in this part of Turkey is frost-intolerant during its flowering and ripening stages. Generally, the unripe almond is eaten raw, dipped in salt, but it is also delicious cooked. The green almond is in season in April. If this fruit is left on the tree to ripen, its green shell hardens.

Grilled Gökova shrimp with creamed sweetcorn soup

For the sweetcorn soup

6 cobs of sweetcorn (corn)

2 onions

1 clove of garlic

50 g (1.75 oz/½ stick) butter

Olive oil

1 bay leaf

Salt

2 litres (68 fl oz/2 quarts)
   water

Freshly ground black pepper

1 sprig of oregano

50 ml (2 fl oz/¼ cup) cream

For the shrimp

8 Gökova shrimp (or fresh
   shrimp or prawns; or try
   crab instead)

Olive oil

Salt

Freshly ground black pepper

2 spring onions (scallions)

4 SERVINGS

Preparation of the sweetcorn soup

When buying sweetcorn (corn), it's important to choose the right variety. I always buy the ears in their husks as exposed corn loses its freshness. If I buy hybrid corn, it becomes evident after cooking as it sticks to your teeth; if it isn't, it doesn't.

Ask the market stallholder to strip a few ears. If they look right, then the rest are likely to be good, too. I prefer sweetcorn (corn) with small kernels that do not shine like pearls, and with thin husks.

After husking the corn, I boil the ears in a large saucepan for 1-1.5 hours. Salt added while boiling makes the corn tough, so I prefer to add it while I cook the soup. I separate the kernels from the cobs with a knife. I slice the onions. Since I am going to mix the soup in a blender later, the size of the onion slices does not matter. I peel the garlic and chop it finely.

I heat some butter and olive oil in a saucepan over a low flame. I mix the butter with the oil to keep it from burning because I don't want it to change colour. I add the onion, garlic and the bay leaf.

Then, to release the juice from the onion, I add salt. I add the sweetcorn (corn) kernels to the sautéed onion and garlic. I boil the water in a separate saucepan and then add it to the sweetcorn (corn) and onion mixture. Adding freshly ground black pepper and a sprig of oregano, I simmer the soup for half an hour.

The starch in the sweetcorn (corn) thickens the soup, which I blend with a blender and I add a pinch of salt. Before serving, I add cream and bring it to the boil.

I don't like soups to be lump-free and completely smooth, so I recommend serving them as they come. However, if I am serving soup in shot glasses at a large reception, or I want a flawless presentation, I strain the soup.

Grilled Gökova shrimp with creamed sweetcorn soup (continued)

Preparation of the shrimp

The season for the most delicious Gökova shrimp is between April and early June. You need large shrimp for this recipe, so in a kilo (2 lb 4 oz) you should have about 12 x 10-cm (4-in)-long shrimps, from which you choose 8. I shell the raw shrimp and remove their heads. You can leave their tails on, if you prefer. I take a thin, pointed knife and I open the body of the shelled shrimp and remove the intestines, which appear as a long black line (or, sometimes, green or dark brown). I combine the shrimp with olive oil, salt, freshly ground black pepper and spring onions (scallions), which I cut lengthwise. Then I cook the shrimp for only 5 minutes on each side on a preheated grill, ensuring that their insides remain juicy.

The flavour of the shrimp varies with the length of cooking: overcooked shrimp is dry and lacks flavour.

Preparing the plate

I serve 2 grilled shrimp with 2 ladles of corn soup in a bowl.

Finally, a sprinkling of spring onion (scallions) enhances the presentation of the dish.

Flavours that complement shrimp

Rocket, avocado, red pepper, spring onion (scallion), coriander, garlic, lemon, rosemary, tomatoes and vinegar

Casserole of Datça tomatoes, aubergines, *köy peyniri* and fresh herbs

2 Datça tomatoes, large
(or vine tomatoes)
2 cloves of garlic
Extra-virgin olive oil
4 sprigs of fresh oregano
Salt
Freshly ground black pepper
1 bunch of fresh basil
2 long, thin aubergines
(eggplants)
Salt
200 g (7 oz) fresh *köy peyniri* *
(or try fresh buffalo
mozzarella)

4 SERVINGS

Preparing the tomatoes

I slice the tomatoes into ½-cm (¼-in)-thick rounds and I mix them in with crushed garlic, olive oil, salt and freshly ground black pepper. I chop the fresh basil and oregano and, after adding them to the tomatoes, I set the mixture aside to marinate for 15-30 minutes.

Preparing the aubergines

I cut the aubergines (eggplants) lengthwise into 5-mm (¼-in)-thick strips. After adding a pinch of salt to each one, I let them sit in a sieve. The salt draws out the bitter juices of the aubergines (eggplant). I then run water over the aubergine (eggplant) strips and pat them dry with a paper towel. I remove the tomatoes from the marinade and put them on a plate and I marinate the aubergines (eggplant) for 15-30 minutes in the same marinade.

Baking

The number of earthenware casserole dishes you need depends on their size, but you will probably need two or four. I layer two slices each of tomato, aubergine (eggplant) and cheese, in that order, so that, in the smaller pots, they form a rising cylinder. I bake them in 160-180°C (320-350°F) for 6-8 minutes and then serve. You can easily adapt this to larger pots.

* *village cheese, a fresh, semi-soft and not very salty cheese from cow's/goat's milk*

Aubergine stuffed with stewed lamb

2 onions
Olive oil
1 bay leaf
1 kg (2 lb 4 oz) leg of lamb,
    boneless
2 cloves of garlic
2 tomatoes
Salt
2 sprigs of fresh oregano
50 g (1.75 oz/½ stick) butter
1 bunch of parsley
4 small, plump, home-grown
    aubergines (eggplant)
Hazelnut oil for frying

4 SERVINGS

Lamb bought between the end of January and the beginning of March is ideal for this dish. I dice the leg of lamb finely (your butcher can do this for you if you prefer). Using a large pan, I sauté the onions, sliced lengthways, in some olive oil, adding the bay leaf and, 1 or 2 minutes later, the meat. I use a wooden spoon to stir the meat and I turn up the heat to release the meat's juices. As the meat's juices are absorbed by the mixture, I turn down the heat.

Once the juice of the meat has been released, I add the crushed garlic, the tomatoes (peeled and diced), salt and oregano, and cook the mixture for about 1.5 hours, until the meat has become extremely soft. After the meat has cooked, I add diced cold butter and finely chopped parsley and mix.

Preparing the aubergines (eggplant)

I carefully select small, plump aubergines (eggplant). I prick the aubergines (eggplant) and drop them into the hazelnut oil, which is deep enough to half submerge them and is preheated to 180°C (350°F). I cook them until they gain a soft texture, about 4 minutes each side. Once cooked, I pat them dry with a paper towel and slice each one lengthwise to make a pocket for the stuffing.

I mash the flesh of the aubergines (eggplant) and I put the stewed lamb inside. Then I bake the whole for 10 minutes at 180°C (350°F/Gas 4). I serve them directly from the oven.

This is a popular dish at my restaurant, especially with rice seasoned with herbs.

Fish soup

For the fish stock
800 g–1 kg (1 lb 12 oz–
   2 lb 4 oz) black
   scorpionfish (or gurnard)
1 onion
1 leek
1 celeriac
1 bay leaf
Peppercorn
100 ml (3.5 fl oz/scant
   ½ cup) white wine
2 litres (68 fl oz/2 quarts)
   water
Salt

For the soup
1 leek
1 celery stick
50 g (1.75 oz/½ stick) butter
2 potatoes

To thicken the soup
1 egg yolk
Juice of 1 lemon

4 SERVINGS

Preparation of the fish stock

Black scorpionfish barbs are poisonous, so it is best if your fishmonger prepares these fish for you. After thoroughly washing them, I put the fish in a pan with a whole onion, chopped leek, celeriac (peeled and diced), the bay leaf, and the peppercorn. I add the white wine and the cold water to the pan and, after adding salt, I simmer the mixture for 30-45 minutes.

Preparation of the soup

I slice the leek and celery stick and I dice the potatoes. I sauté the leek in butter in a medium-sized saucepan. I strain the fish stock and add it to the saucepan and begin cooking. Ten minutes later, I add the potatoes and, while they are cooking, I begin de-boning the fish and I add the meat and the celery stick to the boiling soup.

Preparation of the thickener

If, like me, you like your soup thick and with a sour edge, you can prepare an egg sauce. In a separate bowl, I mix the egg yolk with lemon juice. Then I take a ladle of boiling soup and gradually add it to the egg mixture. After adding a second ladle of soup, I stir the mixture well. Finally, I take this warmed mixture and add it to the soup and bring it to the boil. If you add the egg yolk and lemon juice mixture directly to the soup, the egg yolk cooks and separates in the soup.

Another way of thickening the soup is to puree the vegetables with a hand blender before adding them to the soup, which allows you to dispense with the egg sauce.

FISH ALTERNATIVES
You can use large-scaled scorpionfish or
gurnard in place of black scorpionfish,
as well as the heads of such large fish as
grouper, leerfish, haibut, cod and yellowtail.

Marinated lamb spare ribs

1 kg (2 lb 4 oz) lamb spare
   ribs (not separated)
1 onion
3 cloves of garlic
Salt
50 ml (2 fl oz/scant ¼ cup)
   olive oil
Worcestershire sauce
Tabasco sauce
Ground red pepper
2 sprigs of rosemary
10 g (¼ oz/1½ tsp)
   carob molasses
   (or molasses)
10 g (¼ oz/1½ tsp)
   oregano honey
   (or honey)

4 SERVINGS (6 RIBS PER PERSON)

Young lamb bought between February and April has a light smell and is tastier than that bought later. Ribs from the lamb common to Thrace will give you the best results. You should insist on buying the spare ribs joined rather than separated one from another, as they are commonly sold.

Preparing the marinade

I grate the onion because I want to get as much juice out of it as possible. I crush the garlic with a pinch of salt using a pestle and mortar. Then I put the onion and garlic in a bowl and pour a little olive oil over them. I fork in 3-5 drops of Worcestershire sauce, 3-5 drops of Tabasco sauce (if you like spicy flavours, add more), ground red pepper, finely chopped rosemary, molasses and honey.

I smother the ribs with this marinade, using my hands to ensure that all parts are thoroughly covered. If you have time, let the ribs sit in the refrigerator for 3-5 hours; if you don't have time, let them stand for 30-45 minutes at room temperature.

I prepare a charcoal grill and I don't let it get too hot because I want the ribs to brown slowly. If you prepare your own grill, spread ashes over the burning charcoal to moderate the temperature and, when you want to make the heat stronger, use tongs to lift the coals out of the ash.

I clean the grill with a brush while it is heating up. Then, after drizzling olive oil over the ribs, I place them on the grill and cook both sides until they are well-done. I cleaver the ribs into groups of 3.

This marinade can be used for all kinds of lamb dishes. Ribs are fatty, so they can tolerate more intense flavours.

Pink tomato and *köy ekmeği* salad

¼ of a loaf of *köy ekmeği* *
   (or flat bread of pitta)
2 large pink tomatoes
   (or heirloom or heritage
   tomaotes)
1 bunch of fresh mint
½ bunch of parsley
2 spring onions (scallions)
150 g (5.5 oz) white cheese,
   fatty (or feta)
30 ml (1 oz/2 tbsp) grape
   vinegar
Extra-virgin olive oil
Salt
Freshly ground black pepper

2-4 SERVINGS

Köy ekmeği * (or flat bread or pitta) is denser than the usual bread available in shops. There is less yeast in it, so it doesn't rise as high as other breads. It's more like German breads in that it is moist and dense. Having less yeast and a higher density, slightly stale village bread makes good toast. However, you can use wholegrain bread, buns or even normal white bread for this recipe.

I slice the *köy ekmeği*, which is round, from the centre outwards. The thinner the slice, the more easily it can be eaten, so I take pains to make the slices only 2-3 mm (¹⁄₁₆-⅛ in) thick. I also cut the slices into lengths of no more than 8 cm (3¼ in). I dry the slices for 20-25 minutes in an oven heated to 120°C (248°F).

I dice the tomatoes, complete with their skins and seeds, and I chop the mint and parsley finely. I slice the spring onions (scallions) obliquely and thinly. I put the pieces of bread, then the tomato, then the herbs into a bowl, and then I crumble the white cheese (or feta) on top.

In a separate bowl, I mix the vinegar, olive oil, salt and black pepper, and pour the mixture over the ingredients in the other bowl. Being careful not to crush the tomatoes, I mix the ingredients well and then serve.

This salad will retain its flavour for half an hour, after which the bread will absorb the sauce and become soft, and the salad will deteriorate.

* *village bread, a simple flat bread prepared on a hot plate, not baked*

Baked sea bream with capers and olives

4 sea bream,
    each 400 g (14 oz)
Olive oil
Salt
Freshly ground black pepper
20 black olives
1 red onion
10 cherry tomatoes
10 caper berries
1 handful of fresh oregano

4 SERVINGS

I prefer grilling gilt-head sea bream to baking it and I like it most when the outside of the fish is crispy-brown and it is served with vegetables.

After gutting the bream, I wash it. I dry the fish with a paper towel and then coat the whole fish with olive oil. After rubbing salt and freshly ground black pepper into the fish, I put it aside. It is important that the salt and black pepper are absorbed right into the fish. If the black olives are salty, I soak them in cold water. I pip the olive. I peel the red onion and slice it into rings. I leave the tomatoes whole.

I first place the fish on an oven tray, and then add black olives, red onion, cherry tomatoes, caper berries and fresh oregano. I drizzle some oil over the top and then cover the tray with foil. I bake the covered fish at 160°C (320°F) for 10 minutes and then I bake it uncovered for another 10 minutes. While it is baking, I baste the fish with the vegetable juice and oil.

CAPER BERRIES
We are all familiar with the caper buds sold in small glass jars at markets. But what we use in this recipe is not the buds but the berries—the olive-sized seed the caper produces after flowering. The bush, *Capparis spinosa*, that produces this fruit is abundant on the Datça Peninsula and on the Aegean coast.
If you happen to be in this area at the end of summer, you can pick capers and pickle them. They last a long time. It is difficult to find caper berries in the market, so you can also use the buds in this recipe. Don't forget to wash the contents of jars before using them.

Grilled red mullet and warm cannellini bean puree with lemon rind

For the bean puree
500 g (1 lb 2 oz)
    cannellini beans
1 bay leaf
2 litres (68 fl oz/2 quarts)
    water
Freshly ground black pepper
Juice and rind of 1 lemon
½ bunch of dill
Extra-virgin olive oil
Salt

For the red mullet
½ kg (1 lb 2 oz) red mullet
Olive oil
Sea salt
Freshly ground black pepper
4 spring onions (scallions)

4 SERVINGS

Preparation of the bean puree

I soak the beans overnight. Then I drain the water and put the beans in a saucepan with fresh cold water, a bay leaf and freshly ground black pepper. I boil the beans on a high heat until they are well-cooked. When cooking legumes, I don't add salt because it slows down the cooking process and I don't cover the pan.

I drain the boiled beans and, while they are still warm, I add lemon juice, lemon rind and salt, and puree them with a hand blender. I drizzle olive oil over the puree and stir. I chop the dill finely and add it to the puree.

I also love serving this bean puree with garlic instead of lemon juice and with rosemary as a complement to lamb.

Cooking the red mullet

If the red mullet are large, you can fillet them; if they are small, you can grill (or broil) them as is. Still, I prefer fish that I am going to grill not to be too small. If you make fillets out of the fish and grill them, they cook quickly, so you should keep your eye on them.

I rub the fish with oil, salt and black pepper. I bring the grill (or use a broiler) to a high heat and, while I wait for it to heat up, I clean it by rubbing the cooking surface with lemon juice or an onion. Then I place the fish on the hot grill and, when the fish are nearly cooked, I place spring onion (scallion) on the grill. I make sure that the fish remain moist.

Preparing the serving plates

I place one spoonful of bean puree on the plates and then the fish on top of the puree and top the whole dish off with the cooked spring onion (scallion).

RED MULLET
In summer, red mullet lives in sandy, shallow water along the coasts of the Aegean, Mediterranean, Marmara and Black Seas. They migrate north as summer approaches and return south as winter looms. These fish have plump stomachs, red spines, flanks that range in colour between pink and red, and white bellies. They are delicious both fried and grilled. One red mullet added to a fish soup enhances its aroma.

mallow *78, 122*
mastic *68, 102*
melon *48*
minced meat *50, 56*
mint *28, 48, 110, 147, 150, 180, 196, 206, 248, 256, 272*
molasses *30, 42, 76, 96, 270*
monkfish *120*
mushroom *184, 206*
mussel *70, 128, 138*
mustard *50, 114, 120, 148, 166, 170, 202, 223*

new potatoes *26, 30, 80, 142, 223*
noodle *186, 244*

octopus *44, 138*
olives *26, 58, 88, 112, 114, 118, 211, 237, 274*
orange *28, 44, 58, 68, 120, 138, 164, 202, 228, 234, 246*
oregano *182*
oregano flowers *218*
oxtail *25*
ox-tongue *142, 223*

parsley *44, 50, 70, 74, 80, 102, 110, 112, 114, 128, 138, 142, 147, 164, 180, 184, 196, 202, 223, 226, 244, 246, 256, 262, 266, 272*
peach *48, 172, 190, 216*
pear *32, 76, 238*
peas *98, 206*
pine nuts *28, 56, 122, 194, 234, 226*
pink tomatoes *272*
pizza *36, 118*
pomegranates *22*
pomegranate syrup *22, 72, 180*
potatoes *26, 30, 46, 60, 70, 80, 142, 144, 223, 268*
pumpkin *78, 116*
purslane *18, 22, 72, 109, 114, 124, 140, 147, 180*

quail *184*
quince *162, 238*

rack of lamb *26*
rakı 128
raspberry *216, 228*
red bell pepper *44, 50, 56, 96, 102, 112, 124, 136, 186, 262, 270*
  fresh *194, 214*
red grouper *92*
red mullet *276*
red onion *50, 88, 110, 118, 192, 226, 274*
red wine *42, 44, 120, 182*
rocket *22, 32, 44, 50, 96, 114, 147, 208*
rosemary *20, 26, 30, 42, 72, 112, 114, 120, 160, 182, 184, 186, 190, 194, 216, 218, 220, 238, 262, 270, 276*

sage *90, 116, 244*
samphire *234, 246*
sardines *211, 226*
satsumas *147*
scorpionfish *202, 268*
sea bass *138, 156, 158, 211, 256*
sesame seeds *170*
shank (lamb) *160*
shrimp *138, 166, 260*
  smoked *76, 164, 166*
sole *80*
sorrel *18, 22, 112, 144, 147*
sour cherry *52, 228*
spare ribs *270*
spinach *18, 22, 36, 78, 114, 122, 144, 222*
spring onions *18, 28, 44, 66, 78, 88, 110, 122, 126, 147, 148, 156, 178, 180, 196, 202, 206, 234, 240, 248, 256, 260, 272*
squid *102, 240*
strawberry *48, 162, 216, 228*
sumac *226*
süzme yoğurt 28, 56, 122, 186, 196
sweetcorn *260*
sweet *lor peyniri 100, 122*

tahini *96, 124, 136, 214*
tarragon *256*

tomato *18, 50, 114, 118, 126, 128, 156, 180, 192, 214, 226, 237, 262, 264, 266*
  cherry *274*; pink *272*
tulum peyniri 22, 28, 46, 122, 158, 162, 194, 248
turnip greens *122, 226*
tuna *88, 211*

vanilla stick *34*
vine leave *226*
vinegar *32, 60, 90, 112, 122, 126, 140, 148, 150, 208, 214, 248, 262, 272*
vodka *48*

walnuts *72, 148, 162, 164, 172, 208, 244*
wheat *18, 180*
white cherry *34*
white wine *70, 92, 128, 138, 210, 246, 268*
whiting *110*
wine *32, 42, 44, 70, 92, 110, 114, 120, 128, 138, 182, 246, 268*

yufka 56, 122

Measurements		
1 cup		
	water	225 ml
	oil	225 ml
	flour	125 g
	sugar	200 g
1 tablespoon		
	water	15 ml
	oil	15 ml
	flour	9 g
	sugar	16 g
1 egg		57-60 g
1 egg yolk		20-22 g

With my kitchen-team in Kumlubük.